CIMA

Management Level

E2

Managing Perfomance

Exam Practice Kit

For exams from 4 November 2019 to January 2021

Sixth edition 2019

ISBN 9781 5097 2998 2
e-ISBN 9781 5097 3193 0

British Library Cataloguing-in-Publication Data
A catalogue record for this book
is available from the British Library

Published by

BPP Learning Media Ltd
BPP House, Aldine Place, 142/144 Uxbridge Road
London W12 8AA

www.bpp.com/learningmedia

Printed in the United Kingdom

Your learning materials, published by BPP
Learning Media Ltd, are printed on paper
obtained from traceable, sustainable sources.

We are grateful to the Chartered Institute of
Management Accountants for allowing us to
reproduce extracts from the CIMA exam blueprint.
An up-to-date version of the full blueprint is
available at
www.cimaglobal.com/examblueprints.

Contents

Question and answer index

Using your BPP Exam Practice Kit

One of the key criteria for achieving exam success is question practice. There is generally a direct correlation between candidates who study all topics and practise exam questions and those who are successful in their real exams. This Kit gives you ample opportunity for such practice throughout your preparations for your OT exam.

All questions in your exam are compulsory and all the component learning outcomes will be examined so you must **study the whole syllabus**. Selective studying will limit the number of questions you can answer and hence reduce your chances of passing. It is better to go into the exam knowing a reasonable amount about most of the syllabus rather than concentrating on a few topics to the exclusion of the rest.

Practising as many exam-style questions as possible will be the key to passing this exam. You must do questions under **timed conditions**.

Breadth of question coverage

Questions will cover the whole of the syllabus so you must study all the topics in the syllabus.

The weightings in the table below indicate the approximate proportion of study time you should spend on each topic, and is related to the number of questions per syllabus area in the exam.

E2 Managing Performance Syllabus topics	Weighting
A Business Models and Value Creation	30%
B Manging People Performance	40%
C Managing Projects	30%

(CIMA exam blueprint, 2019)

Examination structure

The Objective Test exam

Pass mark	70%
Format	Computer-based assessment
Duration	90 minutes
Number of questions	60
Marking	No partial marking – each question marked correct or incorrect All questions carry the same weighting (ie same marks)
Weighting	As per syllabus areas All representative task statements from the examination blueprint will be covered
Question Types	Multiple choice Multiple response Drag and drop Gap fill Hot spot
Booking availability	On demand
Results	Immediate

What the examiner means

The table below has been prepared by CIMA to further help you interpret the syllabus and learning outcomes and the meaning of questions.

You will see that there are five skills levels you may be expected to demonstrate, ranging from Remembering and Understanding to Evaluation. CIMA Certificate subjects only use levels 1 to 3, but in CIMA's Professional qualification the entire hierarchy will be used.

Skills level		Verbs used	Definition
Level 5	Evaluation *The examination or assessment of problems, and use of judgment to draw conclusions*	Advise	Counsel, inform or notify
		Assess	Evaluate or estimate the nature, ability or quality of
		Evaluate	Appraise or assess the value of
		Recommend	Propose a course of action
		Review	Assess and evaluate in order, to change if necessary
		Select	Choose an option or course of action after consideration of the alternatives

Skills level		Verbs used	Definition
Level 4	**Analysis** The examination and study of the interrelationships of separate areas in order to identify causes and find evidence to support inferences	Align	Arrange in an orderly way
		Analyse	Examine in detail the structure of
		Communicate	Share or exchange information
		Compare and contrast	Show the similarities and/or differences between
		Develop	Grow and expand a concept
		Discuss	Examine in detail by argument
		Examine	Inspect thoroughly
		Monitor	Observe and check the progress of
		Prioritise	Place in order of priority or sequence for action
		Produce	Create or bring into existence
Level 3	**Application** The use or demonstration of knowledge, concepts or techniques	Apply	Put to practical use
		Calculate	Ascertain or reckon mathematically
		Conduct	Organise and carry out
		Demonstrate	Prove with certainty or exhibit by practical means
		Determine	Ascertain or establish exactly by research or calculation
		Perform	Carry out, accomplish, or fulfil
		Prepare	Make or get ready for use
		Reconcile	Make or prove consistent/compatible
		Record	Keep a permanent account of facts, events or transactions
		Use	Apply a technique or concept

Skills level		Verbs used	Definition
Level 1/2	**Remembering and understanding** The perception and comprehension of the significance of an area utilising knowledge gained	Define	Give the exact meaning of
		Describe	Communicate the key features of
		Distinguish	Highlight the differences between
		Explain	Make clear or intelligible/state the meaning or purpose of
		Identify	Recognise, establish or select after consideration
		Illustrate	Use an example to describe or explain something
		List	Make a list of
		Recognise	Identify/recall
		State	Express, fully or clearly, the details/facts of
		Outline	Give a summary of
		Understand	Comprehend ideas, concepts and techniques

(CIMA exam blueprint, 2019)

How to pass

Good exam technique

The best approach to the computer-based assessment (CBA)

You're not likely to have a great deal of spare time during the CBA itself, so you must make sure you don't waste a single minute.

You should:

1   Click 'Next' for any that have long scenarios or are very complex and return to these later

2   When you reach the 60th question, use the Review Screen to return to any questions you skipped past or any you flagged for review

Here's how the tools in the exam will help you to do this in a controlled and efficient way.

The 'Next' button

What does it do? This will move you on to the next question whether or not you have completed the one you are on.

When should I use it? Use this to move through the exam on your first pass through if you encounter a question that you suspect is going to take you a long time to answer. The Review Screen (see below) will help you to return to these questions later in the exam.

The 'Flag for Review' button

What does it do? This button will turn the icon yellow and when you reach the end of the exam questions you will be told that you have flagged specific questions for review. If the exam time runs out before you have reviewed any flagged questions, they will be submitted as they are.

When should I use it? Use this when you've answered a question but you're not completely comfortable with your answer. If there is time left at the end, you can quickly come back via the Review Screen (see below), but if time runs out at least it will submit your current answer. Do not use the Flag for Review button too often or you will end up with too long a list to review at the end. Important note –studies have shown that you are usually best to stick with your first instincts!

The Review Screen

What does it do? This screen appears after you click 'Next' on the 60th question. It shows you any incomplete questions and any you have flagged for review. It allows you to jump back to specific questions **or** work through all your incomplete questions **or** work through all your flagged for review questions.

When should I use it? As soon as you've completed your first run through the exam and reached the 60th question. The very first thing to do is to work through all your incomplete questions as they will all be marked as incorrect if you don't submit an answer for these in the remaining time. Importantly, this will also help to pick up any questions you thought you'd completed but didn't answer properly (eg you only picked two answer options in a multi-response question that required three answers to be selected). After you've submitted answers for all your incomplete questions you should use the Review Screen to work through all the questions you flagged for review.

The different Objective Test question types

Passing your CBA is all about demonstrating your understanding of the technical syllabus content. You will find this easier to do if you are comfortable with the different types of Objective Test questions that you will encounter in the CBA, especially if you have a practised approach to each one.

You will find yourself continuously practising these styles of questions throughout your Objective Test programme. This way you will check and reinforce your technical knowledge at the same time as becoming more and more comfortable with your approach to each style of question.

Multiple choice

Standard multiple choice items provide four options. One option is correct and the other three are incorrect. Incorrect options will be plausible, so you should expect to have to use detailed, syllabus-specific knowledge to identify the correct answer rather than relying on common sense.

Multiple response

A multiple response item is the same as a multiple choice question, except **more than one** response is required. You will normally (but not always) be told how many options you need to select.

Drag and drop

Drag and drop questions require you to drag a 'token' onto a pre-defined area. These tokens can be images or text. This type of question is effective at testing the order of events, labelling a diagram or linking events to outcomes.

Gap fill

Gap fill (or 'fill in the blank') questions require you to type a short numerical response. You should carefully follow the instructions in the question in terms of how to type your answer – eg the correct number of decimal places.

Hot spot

These questions require you to identify an area or location on an image by clicking on it. This is commonly used to identify a specific point on a graph or diagram.

A final word on time management

Time does funny things in an exam!

Scientific studies have shown that humans have great difficulty in judging how much time has passed if they are concentrating fully on a challenging task (which your CBA should be!).

You can try this for yourself. Have a go at, say, five questions for your paper, and notice what time you start at. As soon as you finish the last question try to estimate how long it took you and then compare to your watch. The majority of us tend to underestimate how quickly time passes and this can cost you dearly in a full exam if you don't take steps to keep track of time.

So, the key thing here is to set yourself sensible milestones, and then get into the habit of regularly checking how you are doing against them:

- You need to develop an internal warning system – 'I've now spent more than three minutes on this one calculation – this is too long and I need to move on!' (less for a narrative question!)

- Keep your milestones in mind (eg approximately 30 questions done after 45 mins). If you are a distance from where you should be then adjust your pace accordingly. This usually means speeding up but can mean slowing down a bit if needs be, as you may be rushing when you don't need to and increasing the risk of making silly mistakes.

A full exam will be a mix of questions you find harder and those you find easier, and in the real CBA the order is randomised, so you could get a string of difficult questions right at the beginning of your exam. Do not be put off by this – they should be balanced later by a series of questions you find easier.

Objective test questions

1 The ecosystems of organisations

1.1 **Which of the following factors concerning 'drivers of customer demand in the digital age' is being described in the statement below?**

'Customers demand products and services that are tailored to their needs.'

- ○ Seamless experience across channels
- ○ Peer-review and advocacy
- ○ Contextualised interactions
- ○ Transparency

1.2 Nisar regularly makes use of the Electronics-R-Us website, a product comparison platform which provides detailed customer reviews on the latest technology devices, including mobile phones and tablet computers. Electronics-R-Us has become the go-to resource for users of the latest technologies keen on getting feedback left by previous purchasers of electronic products.

Which of the following factors concerning 'drivers of customer demand in the digital age' does the service provided by Electronics-R-Us embody?

- ○ Contextualised interactions
- ○ Seamless experience across channels
- ○ Transparency
- ○ Peer-review and advocacy

1.3 Gary is a Finance Manager working at Bell Co. Gary has just come out of a meeting with other departmental managers which discussed the need for Bell Co to keep ahead of customer expectations. The R&D Manager emphasised the need to avoid complacency in terms of the range of products that Bell Co offers.

During the meeting, Gary advocated the importance of Bell Co ensuring that its products were designed in such a way that they could be distributed more widely and offered on multiple platforms.

Which approach to keeping ahead of customer expectations is Gary advocating?

- ○ Brand atomisation
- ○ Design thinking
- ○ Prototyping
- ○ Experiential pilots

1.4 Traditional regulatory frameworks are being challenged by the emergence of ecosystems in a number of ways.

Which TWO of the following factors have been identified as challenging traditional regulatory frameworks?

☐ Need for new technological infrastructures

☐ Innovators find 'back doors'

☐ Speed of change

☐ Workforces need to be reimagined

☐ Insufficient numbers of regulatory staff

1.5 Organisations have historically competed for control of markets and industries through their interactions with a broad number of stakeholder groups.

Complete the definition of stakeholders using the terms below:

Stakeholders are people, groups or organisations that can affect or be affected by the

[_____] or [_____] of an organisation. Each stakeholder group has

different [_____] about what it wants, and therefore different [_____]

upon the organisation.

Picklist:

expectations
policies
claims
actions
controls
interests
strategies

1.6 Traditional business environments can be analysed using Porter's five forces model.

What does Porter's five forces model show?

○ The five forces which affect one particular business

○ The five forces which influence the state of competition in a given industry

○ The five forces which make up the power of substitutes in a given industry

○ The five forces which influence the state of competition in a given market

1.7 Company A provides high speed train services between London and Paris. Company B operates airline services between London and Paris.

Which of Porter's five forces characterises the provision of the services offered by Company A and Company B?

○ Threat of new entrants

○ Competitive rivalry

○ Threat of substitutes

○ Power of suppliers

BPP
LEARNING
MEDIA

1.8 **Complete IBM's definition of ecosystems using the terms below:**

Ecosystems comprise a [   ] of [   ] enterprises and [   ] aimed at creating and allocating business [   ].

Picklist:

relationships
value
interdependent
complex web
environments
interactions
resources

1.9 Davidson et al highlight that mutuality is a fundamental component in the concept of ecosystems.

Which of the following is Davidson et al's definition of mutuality?

○ The co-ordination, arrangement and management of complex environments

○ Linkages across the ecosystem environment which connect data, information and knowledge

○ An enhanced level of co-ordination with formally or informally shared ideals, standards or goals

○ Speed and direction of exchanges of value among participants

---

1.10 ABC Co is an ecosystem participant. ABC Co-operates an online auction website which brings together millions of different parties from around the world. Users of the ABC Co website are able to enter into transactions for the exchange of goods with one another. ABC Co does not buy or sell goods itself.

How would ABC Co be classified in terms of the role that it undertakes in its ecosystem?

○ Virtual retailer

○ Digital business platform provider

○ Digital operating model provider

○ IT hardware provider

1.11 In traditional markets, value creation can be analysed using Porter's value chain model.

Which of the following is NOT one of the support activities per Porter's value chain?

○ Marketing and sales

○ Technology development

○ Human resources management

○ Procurement

1.12 Which of the following correctly shows the order of the primary activities per Porter's value chain model?

- ○ Inbound logistics, marketing and sales, service, operations, outbound logistics
- ○ Inbound logistics, service, operations, outbound logistics, marketing and sales
- ○ Inbound logistics, operations, outbound logistics, marketing and sales, service
- ○ Inbound logistics, outbound logistics, marketing and sales, service, operations

---

1.13 Which of the following options defines value creation in ecosystem environments according to Davidson et al?

- ○ One-to-one process of exchange
- ○ Everyone-to-one process of exchange
- ○ Business-to-business process of exchange
- ○ Everyone-to-everyone process of exchange

1.14 Technology is driving the emergence of ecosystem environments which have certain features.

Which TWO of the following are features of modern ecosystem environments?

- ☐ Simple
- ☐ Smart
- ☐ Open
- ☐ Extendable
- ☐ Accessible

1.15 Which of Davidson et al's features of ecosystem participants is being described in the following statement?

'The ability of participants to extend their activities through the ecosystem environment.'

- ○ Role
- ○ Rules
- ○ Reach
- ○ Range

1.16 **Which of Davidson et al's features of ecosystem interactions is being described in the following statement?**

'The speed and direction of exchanges of value among participants.'

- ○ Course of interactions
- ○ Transactions
- ○ Rules
- ○ Connections

1.17 Davidson et al identified four distinct roles that an ecosystem participant can take.

Which THREE of the following were roles identified by Davidson et al that a participant in an ecosystem might take?

- ☐ Technology provider
- ☐ Value provider
- ☐ Experience provider
- ☐ Digital provider
- ☐ Process provider
- ☐ Platform provider

1.18 Davidson et al identified four distinct roles that an ecosystem participant can take.

Which of Davidson et al's four distinct roles is being described in the following example?

'A company operating a mobile app which aims to improve the ease for customers of making dinner reservations at a number of restaurants in an ecosystem.'

- ○ Asset provider
- ○ Experience provider
- ○ Process provider
- ○ Value provider

1.19 Davidson et al identified four distinct roles that an ecosystem participant can take.

Which of Davidson et al's four distinct roles is being described in the following example?

'A company offering customers bespoke interior design services to meet a customer's specific needs.'

- ○ Experience provider
- ○ Platform provider
- ○ Asset provider
- ○ Process provider

1.20   Davidson et al identified four types of ecosystem. Each type of ecosystem classification is
        dependent on the extent of orchestration and degree of complexity in the environment.

        **Which type of ecosystem has a low degree of complexity and loose (limited) degree of
        orchestration?**

        ○   Lion's pride

        ○   Shark tank

        ○   Wolf pack

        ○   Hornet's nest

1.21   Davidson et al identified four types of ecosystem. Each type of ecosystem classification is
        dependent on the extent of orchestration and degree of complexity in the environment.

        **Which type of ecosystem has a low degree of complexity and tight (high) degree of
        orchestration?**

        ○   Wolf pack

        ○   Lion's pride

        ○   Hornet's nest

        ○   Shark tank

1.22   Davidson et al identified four types of ecosystem. Each type of ecosystem classification is
        dependent on the extent of orchestration and degree of complexity in the environment.

        **Which of the following are features of a lion's pride ecosystem according to Davidson et
        al?**

        ○   High degree of complexity and tight orchestration

        ○   Low degree of complexity and loose orchestration

        ○   High degree of complexity and loose orchestration

        ○   Low degree of complexity and tight orchestration

2   The elements of business models

2.1   **Complete the definition of the term business model using the terms below:**

       A business model is concerned with how an organisation is ⬚⬚⬚⬚⬚⬚ , the
       ⬚⬚⬚⬚⬚⬚ and ⬚⬚⬚⬚⬚⬚ that it serves, the ⬚⬚⬚⬚⬚⬚ and services
       that it provides, and how it creates ⬚⬚⬚⬚⬚⬚ for stakeholders over time.

       Picklist:

       products
       markets
       structured
       customers
       value
       outputs
       managed
       profit

2.2 According to CIMA there are four stages in the process of value creation.

Which stage is characterised by a focus on the resources and relationships needed, and the activities to be undertaken to be able to develop products and services demanded by stakeholders?

- ○ Deliver value
- ○ Capture value
- ○ Define value
- ○ Create value

2.3 A number of tools exist which can be used by organisations to help them understand the business environments in which they operate.

Which of the following tools would an organisation use to understand the macro-environment?

- ○ Five forces
- ○ PESTEL
- ○ Value chain
- ○ Balanced scorecard

2.4 The increasing use of advanced mobile technologies among the general population has led to an increase in the amount of personal data being held about individuals by large companies. In recent times concerns have been growing among the general population about the use of personal data by companies. In response, the government has introduced new data protection regulations aimed at restricting the volume and types of data that companies can hold about individuals.

In which TWO sections of a PESTEL analysis would the above matter be recorded?

- ☐ Environmental
- ☐ Legal
- ☐ Economic
- ☐ Social
- ☐ Technological

2.5 In the lead up to a general election in the country of Ceeland, the main political opposition party is promising to cut the rate of corporation tax paid by digital platform providers in a bid to attract investment in the country.

In which section of a PESTEL analysis would the cut in the corporation tax be recorded?

- ○ Technological
- ○ Economic
- ○ Environmental
- ○ Legal

2.6 According to CIMA, the VUCA acronym can be used to define rapidly changing business environments.

What does the VUCA acronym stand for?

○ Volatile, uncertain, complex and ambiguous

○ Volatile, unclear, complicated and abstract

○ Volatile, unstable, confusing and ambivalent

○ Volatile, unsuitable, causal, ambitious

2.7 The four perspectives of Kaplan and Norton's balanced scorecard model can be used to help organisations to understand their business model.

One of the four perspectives requires the organisation to address the question 'what processes must we excel at?'

Which balanced scorecard perspective does the above question relate to?

○ Financial perspective

○ Customer perspective

○ Internal business perspective

○ Innovation and learning perspective

2.8 CIMA highlights that the process of ranking and prioritising stakeholders involves ranking stakeholders against three key attributes.

Which of the following are the THREE key attributes?

☐ Influence

☐ Power

☐ Rights

☐ Importance

☐ Urgency

☐ Legitimacy

2.9 A manager at Swift plc is in the process of conducting a stakeholder analysis using Mendelow's power-interest matrix. The manager is trying to determine the attitude of Swift plc's institutional shareholders towards a project to introduce a new piece of payroll software at the company.

In respect of the situation described above, how would Swift Co's institutional shareholders be classified using Mendelow's power-interest matrix?

○ Keep satisfied stakeholder group

○ Keep informed stakeholder group

○ Key players stakeholder group

○ Minimal effort stakeholder group

2.10 CIMA highlights that five main features must connect and align in order to create value.

Which THREE of the following form part of the five main features?

☐ Partners

☐ Relationships

☐ Inputs

☐ Processes

☐ Stakeholders

☐ Resources

2.11 **How would an industry standard piece of IT hardware being used by a company operating in a high-end manufacturing design ecosystem be classified?**

○ As a threshold competence

○ As a threshold resource

○ As a core competence

○ As a unique resource

2.12 **An airline, along with all of its competitors in the same ecosystem, has the right to book landing slots at an airport. How would the right to book the landing slots be classified?**

○ A tangible threshold resource

○ A unique resource

○ An aviation resource

○ An intangible threshold resource

2.13 **How would a patent for a new medicine belonging to an international pharmaceutical company be classified?**

○ As a tangible unique resource

○ As an intangible threshold resource

○ As an intangible unique resource

○ As a tangible threshold resource

2.14   CIMA highlights that five main features must connect and align in order to create value. One of these features is processes.

Complete the definition of the term processes using the terms below:

Organisations need to have in place [＿＿＿＿＿] to turn [＿＿＿＿＿] into [＿＿＿＿＿] as these are its products or services. Processes are effectively the steps that an organisation takes to meet its [＿＿＿＿＿].

Picklist:

inputs
controls
outputs
resources
processes
goals
objectives

2.15   A manufacturer of mobile phones aims to meet its customers' minimum requirements by manufacturing a range of devices with basic functionality. To achieve this, the manufacturer operates an automated production facility. Competing firms manufacture more advanced mobile devices.

How would the manufacturer's automated production facility operations be classified?

○   As a core competence

○   As a threshold resource

○   As a threshold competence

○   As a unique resource

2.16   CIMA highlights that five main features must connect and align in order to create value. One of these features concerns outputs. Outputs are the product, service or experience that are created by an organisation. According to CIMA three attributes make up an organisation's outputs.

Which THREE of the following make up the attributes of an organisation's outputs?

☐   Cost

☐   Amenity

☐   Design

☐   Value

☐   Quality

☐   Price

BPP
LEARNING
MEDIA

2.17 Every market consists of potential customers with different needs and different buying behaviours. As such, customers may be grouped into segments.

One form of segmentation is not based on objective data but instead is based on how people see themselves and their subjective feelings and attitudes towards a particular product or service.

Which type of customer segmentation is being described above?

- ○ Psychographic
- ○ Geographic
- ○ Sociographic
- ○ Demographic

2.18 CIMA highlights that three issues exist which organisations need to consider when capturing value.

Which of the following are the THREE issues highlighted by CIMA?

- ☐ Cost model
- ☐ Profit model
- ☐ Surplus value approach
- ☐ Revenue model
- ☐ Contribution model
- ☐ Distribution of surplus

3 Digital disruption and digital business models

3.1 Volume, Variety, and Velocity are key characteristics of Big Data.

Which other V is associated with the concept of Big Data?

- ○ Veracity
- ○ Validity
- ○ Value
- ○ Viability

3.2 **Which of the following technologies is classified as a 'public form of bookkeeping that uses a digital ledger to allow individuals to share a record of transactions'?**

- ○ FinTech
- ○ Blockchain
- ○ Cryptocurrency
- ○ Digital assets

3.3 John has just read an article on a respected business website which discussed the rise in peer-to-peer lending in the banking sector.

Which disruptive technology is most closely associated with the rise in peer-to-peer lending?

- ○ Blockchain
- ○ Cryptocurrency
- ○ FinTech
- ○ Digital assets

3.4 Alice workers for BTT Co, an online fashion retailer. Alice has noticed that a number of BTT Co's competitors have started to allow customers to pay for their purchases using Bitcoin.

Which type of disruptive technology is Bitcoin an example of?

- ○ The Internet of Me
- ○ Cryptocurrency
- ○ FinTech
- ○ Digital assets

3.5 **An MP3 file is an example of which type of technology?**

- ○ Cryptocurrency
- ○ Digital asset
- ○ Drone technology
- ○ Cloud computing

3.6 The World Economic Forum suggests that there are five trends that business leaders should focus on when determining how best to deal with digital disruption.

Which of these trends places 'users at the centre of a personalised digital experience'?

- ○ Outcome economy
- ○ The Platform (r)evolution
- ○ The internet of me
- ○ The intelligent enterprise

3.7 The World Economic Forum suggest that there are five trends that business leaders should focus on when determining how best to deal with digital disruption.

Which of these trends is concerned with the evolution of platforms which offer opportunities for innovation and faster service delivery?

- ○ The Platform (r)evolution
- ○ Outcome economy
- ○ Workforce reimagined
- ○ The intelligent enterprise

3.8 Sally is the Finance Director at Astra Co. She has just read an article about the growing use of technologies including sensors and tracking devices which are increasingly being embedded in the products and services provided by organisations.

Which of the following terms characterises the use of sensors and tracking devices in products and services?

- ○ Internet of Things
- ○ Cloud computing
- ○ Artificial intelligence
- ○ Automation

3.9 Warren Co is a manufacturer of fashion clothing for men and women. In order to keep its offering relevant to customers, Warren Co is in the process of developing a new business model. As such Warren Co has invested extensively in improving its data analytics capabilities, which will allow it to more easily monitor fashion trends. To maximise the benefits from its enhanced data analytics capabilities Warren Co has hired individuals with expertise in the field of data science. The directors at Warren Co are hopeful that these investments will lead to the development of new fashion products which appeal to customers.

Which of the World Economic Forum's strategies for creating disruptive business models BEST describes the situation involving Warren Co?

- ○ Buy strategy
- ○ Partner strategy
- ○ Incubate/accelerate strategy
- ○ Build strategy

3.10 Zuma Co (Zuma), a sportswear manufacturer, has recently teamed up with Muzic Choice, a music streaming service, to develop a mobile app that matches users' favourite music to the intensity of their workout. The board at Zuma hope to gain a better understanding of how the types of sports clothing and equipment that it develops can be used to complement the technologies (ie mobile apps) that its customers are likely to use in the future.

Which of the World Economic Forum's strategies for creating disruptive business models best describes the situation involving Zuma Co and Muzic Choice?

- ○ Build strategy
- ○ Incubate/accelerate strategy
- ○ Partner strategy
- ○ Invest strategy

3.11   Small Co is a privately owned, recently formed technology company which develops software for the airline industry. Small Co has recently approached Large plc, a multi-national software house, in a bid to gain financial banking to support the development of its latest software package. The board at Large plc have agreed to purchase a small number of shares in Small Co on the grounds that they view Small Co as being an interesting start-up with a lot of potential. Large plc's shareholding is considerably less than would be needed to obtain control over the affairs of Small Co.

Which of the World Economic Forum's strategies for creating disruptive business models best describes the situation involving Small Co and Large plc?

○   Partner strategy

○   Buy strategy

○   Build strategy

○   Invest strategy

3.12   Mac Dermot's, a multi-national chain of fast food restaurants, has recently purchased a small number of shares in Eat Now, a privately owned technology start-up firm, which has developed a mobile restaurant booking app. Although Eat Now has workers with the required technical skills in developing mobile apps, it currently lacks the expertise that it will need to successfully advertise and promote the app. Following its investment in Eat Now, Mac Dermot's board announced its intention to deploy a small team from its own marketing department to help Eat Now promote the restaurant booking app.

Which of the World Economic Forum's strategies for creating disruptive business models best describes the situation involving Mac Dermot's and Eat Now?

○   Build strategy

○   Incubate/accelerate strategy

○   Partner strategy

○   Invest strategy

3.13   The World Economic Forum identified five digital operating models which organisations can use when responding to digital disruption.

Which digital operating model is focused on keeping costs low?

○   Data-powered

○   Skynet

○   Open and Liquid

○   Xtra-Frugal

3.14 The Managing Director at Finn Co has recently attended a conference which explored the concept of digital operating models. The Managing Director is keen to adopt the Skynet digital operating model as identified by the World Economic Forum.

Which THREE of the following strategies should Finn Co seek to embrace in order to adopt the Skynet digital operating model?

☐ Formulate a hub and spoke organisational structure

☐ Improve productivity and flexibility

☐ Develop an ecosystem environment

☐ Empower its customer-facing staff

☐ Formulate a centralised organisational structure

☐ Develop a strong engineer culture with a focus on automation

3.15 Willow plc (Willow) operates a mobile phone app which provides owners of residential property in major European cities with a platform to advertise and facilitate short-term residential lettings to private individuals. Willow's culture emphasises the importance of collaboration. Willow often works with external parties which offer complementary services to its own. One company it works with offers car rental services in the same cities that Willow operates in. Willow and the car rental company often share information about customer bookings and promote each other's services to customers.

Which type of digital operating model has Willow plc adopted using the World Economic Forum's classifications?

○ Xtra-Frugal

○ Data-powered

○ Skynet

○ Open and Liquid

3.16 Nile plc (Nile) is an online book retailer. Nile's Managing Director is emphatic about offering the best levels of service, and Nile's customer-first ethos is central to everything the company does. All staff working in Nile's customer call centre and its online customer support website are empowered to use their initiative to ensure that the customer is kept happy.

Which type of digital operating model has Nile plc adopted using the World Economic Forum's classifications?

○ Xtra-Frugal

○ Customer-centric

○ Skynet

○ Open and Liquid

3.17 Bell Co is a company which allows individuals and businesses alike to order bespoke computers built to their exact requirements. Customers place orders via the Bell Co website. Most customer queries are answered by the chatbot interface on the Bell Co website, which can answer frequently asked questions. Once a customer places an order this is automatically routed to the manufacturing department, where a series of robotic machines build the computer ordered to the customer's specification. Once the computer has been built it is packaged automatically and is delivered on a conveyor belt to Bell Co's warehouse, where it is collected by a courier for delivery to the customer. Bell Co's management team is constantly looking to improve the productivity of its manufacturing operations.

Which type of digital operating model has Bell Co adopted using the World Economic Forum's classifications?

○ Open and Liquid

○ Data-powered

○ Customer-centric

○ Skynet

3.18 Andrew Smith is the CEO of AMB Co, a company which manufactures simple mobile phones (being those with limited functionality). Andrew is keen for AMB Co to develop a range of advanced smart mobile devices which possess cutting edge features to support the latest mobile apps. Andrew is aware that before AMB Co can develop new mobile devices the company will need to foster a digital culture to embrace digital change.

Which TWO of the following actions, according to the World Economic Forum, will AMB Co need to undertake to develop a digital culture?

☐ Permit staff greater freedom to be creative in product development

☐ Ensure that all staff have access to a computer

☐ Encourage staff to challenge existing ways of working

☐ Provide all new staff with an induction which focuses on AMB Co's origins

☐ Appoint a new team leader to oversee the work of the admin team at AMB Co

3.19 Amir has just come out of a business conference where the key note speaker discussed the Seven Steps which the World Economic Forum recommend an organisation follows when creating a digital workforce. Unfortunately, Amir cannot remember all of the Seven Steps and has asked you to review the notes he took during the session to identify those Steps specified by the World Economic Forum.

Which TWO of the following are steps recommended by the World Economic Forum in creating a digital workforce?

☐ Become an employer of choice

☐ Innovate on the periphery

☐ Harmonise environments

☐ Copy successful digital firms

☐ Embrace the concept of scientific management

 BPP LEARNING MEDIA

3.20 Aidan Thomas has identified that a number of competing training providers in the provision of professional accountancy courses have started to hire in digital specialists on short-term contracts to work on projects aimed at facilitating the delivery of online training courses. The digital specialists are working alongside the training providers' own permanent members of staff to deliver the projects.

Which step in the World Economic Forum's Seven Steps for creating a digital workforce does Aidan's observation relate to?

○ Become an employer of choice

○ Integrate on-demand workforce

○ Foster a digital culture

○ Attracting and retaining workers

3.21 Suresh Patel is the owner of Toyz For You, a chain of high street toy shops. Toyz For You was founded by Suresh's family over 50 years ago, and is based in a country where an increasing proportion of shopping is done online. All sales at Toyz For You are made via its 10 branches, as the company does not currently operate a website. Suresh is aware of the impact that digital technologies are having on smaller businesses and is keen to develop Toyz For You's current business model. Suresh is keen to develop a website capable of taking orders online and developing a presence on social media.

Which of the following is an internal factor that Suresh will have to overcome to develop Toyz For You's business model?

○ A lack of interest among customers to purchase toys online from Toyz For You

○ A lack of technical knowledge among Toyz For You's management team about developing an online presence

○ The risk of opposing moves by Toyz For You's competitors

○ The risk that the government introduce an additional tax on toys sold online

3.22 The World Economic Forum suggests that when established organisations decide to disrupt their existing business models, they should follow three steps.

Which of the following is a feature of Step 2 in this process according to the World Economic Forum?

○ Hire digitally savvy individuals

○ Appoint a digital leader

○ Develop the digital skills of the workforce

○ Invest in the latest technologies

3.23   The board of directors at River plc, a large multi-national online retailer, are debating whether to introduce a new technology aimed at making the lives of its customers easier. It has been proposed that River introduce a physical device called the 'Quick' button. The 'Quick' button will be issued to all River customers, allowing them to place an order for an everyday household item that the customer has specifically programmed to the device. When the customer requires the purchase of the item they can simply press the 'Quick' button which raises an order for delivery. The board hope that the 'Quick' button will remove the need for the customer to visit the River website.

Which type of technological development does the 'Quick' button represent?

○   Big data

○   Cloud computing

○   Artificial intelligence

○   Automation

3.24   **Which of the following is NOT a direct advantage of creating a digital workforce?**

○   The ability to enhance existing ways of working

○   The ability to access new customers through digital channels

○   The reduction in recruitment and associated costs

○   The ability to develop new products or services

3.25   The World Economic Forum identified five digital operating models which organisations can use when responding to digital disruption.

Which digital operating model leads to the formation of a decentralised organisational structure?

○   Customer-centric

○   Open and Liquid

○   Skynet

○   Data-powered

---

4   Key concepts in management

4.1   **What is the key contribution of the human relations approach to management?**

○   Awareness of the importance of group dynamics and worker attitudes as an influence on productivity

○   Concern for productivity and efficiency

○   Awareness of the many different variables that influence and constrain a manager's behaviour

○   Proof of a clear link between job satisfaction, worker motivation and business success

---

4.2 Which of the following is NOT one of Mintzberg's three managerial roles?

○ Inspirational

○ Informational

○ Decisional

○ Interpersonal

4.3 Which TWO of the following are part of the Management by Objectives process?

☐ Set a corporate mission statement

☐ Set objectives for the organisation

☐ Manage managers

☐ Determine objectives for key stakeholders

☐ Organise the work

4.4 Handy's Shamrock would be appropriate as an organisational structure for which TWO of the following organisations?

☐ An airline

☐ A sole trader management consultant

☐ A design agency

☐ A sports team

☐ A freelance doctor

4.5 Which theorist's work is associated with motivational and hygiene factors?

○ Fayol

○ Herzberg

○ Drucker

○ Maslow

4.6 Which of the following statements about organic organisations is true?

○ An organisation exists even before it is filled with people.

○ Pay scales are prescribed according to the position or office held in the organisation structure.

○ Procedures ensure that, regardless of who carries out tasks, they should be executed in the same way.

○ There are differences of status, determined by people's greater expertise and experience.

4.7 In her interview, Mary has been told her role involves tasks that are specific to the firm and require firm-specific skills and experience. She will need to be functionally flexible in terms of multi-skilling and even re-skilling, though training will be provided for this.

This type of worker is referred to as:

○ The professional core

○ Peripheral group

○ Flexible labour force

○ Contractual fringe

4.8 **Which THREE of the following are functions of management according to Fayol?**

☐ Planning

☐ Commanding

☐ Communicating

☐ Orchestrating

☐ Controlling

☐ Arranging

4.9 **Bureaucracy is associated with the work of which theorist?**

○ Weber

○ Mayo

○ Herzberg

○ Taylor

4.10 **Monitoring, disseminating information and acting as a spokesperson all form part of which of theorist's work?**

○ Lewin's three-stage model of change

○ The Ashridge Management College's four management styles

○ Mintzberg's three managerial roles

○ French and Raven's sources of power

4.11 Which major sub system, is the more dominant at WPW Company before and after technology was introduced?

Match each of the roles against the description of WPW Company:

At WPW there were small, integrated work groups consisting of a skilled man, his mate and one or two labourers. There was a high degree of autonomy at the work group level. The group was paid for its work as a group.

▼

WPW then introduced new technology creating a need for larger more specialised groups. A single cycle of mechanised production might extend over three shifts, each performing a separate process and made up of 10 to 20 men. Physical dispersion also greatly increased.

▼

Picklist:

Social systems
Technical systems

4.12 Which of the following is NOT a feature of Burns and Stalker's organic organisational form?

- ○ Management is based on consultation and involvement
- ○ Employees recruited from a variety of sources
- ○ Commitment to task achievement exceeds need for obedience
- ○ High degree of task specialisation

4.13 Which TWO of the following are advantages of bureaucracy?

- ☐ Communication is only through established channels, which increases suggestions made
- ☐ They are ideal for standardised, routine tasks
- ☐ Some people are suited to the structured, predictable environments
- ☐ It results in fast decision making
- ☐ They can enhance creativity, initiative and openness to new ideas and ways of doing things

4.14 Sherwood Company employs 6,000 staff. Results from a recent staff survey suggest high levels of dissatisfaction, despite Mr Sherwood himself being a thoroughly decent chap. It is evident that some of the causes are related to hygiene factors and some to motivational factors.

Which THREE of the following causes of dissatisfaction in Sherwood Company represent hygiene factors?

- ☐ Unpleasant working conditions
- ☐ Limited opportunities for career advancement
- ☐ Below market rate salary
- ☐ High levels of supervision and tight control
- ☐ No recognition of high performance
- ☐ Routine and boring work

4.15 McGonagall, the Finance Director, has worked for HSWW for over 20 years and during that period many of her colleagues have commented that she is the best manager they have had and want to imitate her.

Which of the following best indicates the power source this gives McGonagall?

- ○ Coercive
- ○ Referent
- ○ Reward
- ○ Expert

4.16 **Empowerment goes hand in hand with which THREE of the following?**

- ☐ Centralisation
- ☐ Flexibility
- ☐ Increasing middle management
- ☐ Top-down management
- ☐ New technology
- ☐ Delayering

4.17 D I WHY? hardware store recently placed an advertisement for new shop floor staff. Having selected a number of candidates to attend an interview, Joe-Boy, the HR Manager, advises Jessie-May, the departmental manager, of company policy regarding approved interviewing methods. The final decision on which candidate to recruit remains with the respective department manager.

What kind of authority does Joe-Boy have?

- ○ Line authority
- ○ Staff authority
- ○ Functional authority
- ○ Service authority

BPP
LEARNING
MEDIA

4.18 **Match the terms below with the correct level on Maslow's hierarchy of needs:**

- Basic needs
- Esteem needs
- Social needs
- Safety needs
- Self-actualisation

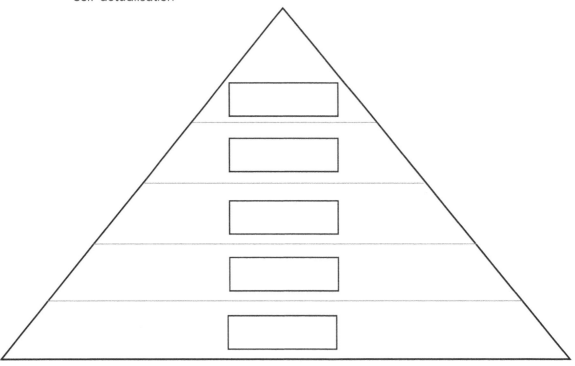

5 Key concepts in leadership

5.1 Dave is the Finance Manager at YTL Co. He has just been asked to oversee a project to upgrade the software used by the finance department. The software to be implemented has already been chosen. None of the current members of the finance team have been involved in the implementation of new software before, with many of them complacent of the need to change. The project is part of YTL Co's new corporate strategy which will involve the company's entire IT infrastructure being improved.

Dave is keen to understand which of Goleman's leadership styles would be MOST appropriate to use when serving as the project manager?

○ Democratic

○ Pacesetting

○ Visionary

○ Commanding

5.2 Daisy is a senior manager at Wow.com. She uses vision, example and persuasion to convince the group to pursue a new purpose. Colleagues have described her as possessing foresight. She understands and empathises with group members' needs, and will empower group members, so as to make the group more effective. She also has good self-understanding.

Daisy would be described as which type of leader?

- ○ Transactional
- ○ Transformational
- ○ Contingency
- ○ Theory X

5.3 Likert described a range of four management styles or 'systems'.

Match the management style to the management behaviour:

The leader has only superficial trust in subordinates, motivates by reward and, though sometimes involving others in problem solving, is basically paternalistic.
[▼]

The leader imposes decisions, never delegates, motivates by threat, has little communication with subordinates and does not encourage teamwork.
[▼]

The leader has confidence in subordinates, who are allowed to make decisions for themselves. Motivation is by reward for achieving goals set by participation, and there is a substantial amount of sharing of ideas, opinions and co-operation.
[▼]

The leader listens to subordinates but controls decision making, motivates by a level of involvement, and will use the ideas and suggestions of subordinates constructively.
[▼]

Picklist:

Participative
Exploitative authoritative
Benevolent authoritative
Consultative

5.4 Stevie Jobbs (Head of HR at Stor-less supermarkets) has observed that different managers across the company's operations adopt very different attitudes to attending corporate meetings. She has recently noted a number of comments made by different managers regarding such meetings.

Match the manager's comment to the correct managerial style:

I attend because it is expected. I either go along with the majority position or avoid expressing my views.	▼
I try to come up with good ideas, and push for a decision as soon as I can get a majority behind me. I don't mind stepping on people if it helps making a sound decision.	▼
I like to be able to support what my boss wants and to recognise the merits of individual effort. When conflict rises, I do a good job of restoring harmony.	▼

Picklist:

1,1 Impoverished
1,9 Country Club
9,1 Task Oriented
5,5 Middle of the road
9,9 Team

5.5 Many Chartered Global Management Accountants serve as leaders in organisations. Although intended for accountants, the CIMA Code of Ethics sets out five fundamental ethical principles which are relevant to the role of leaders in organisations.

Match each principle to its description:

A professional accountant should be straightforward and honest in all professional and business relationships.	▼
A professional accountant should not allow bias, conflict of interest or undue influence of others to override professional or business judgements.	▼
A professional accountant has a continuing duty to maintain professional knowledge and skill and should act diligently and in accordance with applicable technical and professional standards when providing professional services.	▼
A professional accountant should not disclose any information acquired as a result of professional and business relationships without proper and specific authority, unless there is a legal or professional right or duty to disclose.	▼
A professional accountant should comply with relevant laws and regulations, and should avoid any action that discredits the profession.	▼

Picklist:

Confidentiality
Integrity
Professional behaviour
Professional competence and due care
Objectivity

5.6   **Match Lewin's stage of the change process with the relevant activities:**

Identifying those forces resisting change.

▼

Staff participation to help create the necessary 'buy in' to the new status quo

▼

Gradually making the move towards its desired end state

▼

A significant amount of management time will be spent reinforcing the adoption by staff of the new processes

▼

Strengthening the position of those forces driving the need for change

▼

The new state being embedded

▼

Picklist:
Unfreeze
Change
Refreeze

5.7   **Which of the following BEST describes the term leadership?**

○   To challenge things that are taken for granted

○   The process of getting activities completed efficiently and effectively with and through other people.

○   Translating an organisation's overall strategy to stakeholders

○   The ability to get others to follow willingly

5.8   Project W is a severely time-constrained research project and must be completed to high quality standards.

The project staff all have academic qualifications and a wealth of relevant experience.

They are divided into four specialist teams, each working on separate, complex problems.

Each team is headed by an expert in the relevant field.

The project manager has good experience of the general theoretical background to the work being done but ceased to be involved in practical research some years ago.

Which management style would you expect to be LEAST useful to the project manager?

○   Tells

○   Sells

○   Consults

○   Joins

5.9   **What is the central feature of the trait theory of leadership?**

○   Leaders can be taught management skills.

○   Leaders are effective due to the style that they use when interacting with others.

○   Leaders spread the leadership role among a number of individuals in their teams.

○   Leaders are effective due to innate personal characteristics.

5.10 Lewin et al identified three styles of leadership.

Which THREE of the following are the styles of leadership identified by Lewin et al?

☐ Authoritarian

☐ Exploitative authoritative

☐ Theory X

☐ Democratic

☐ Impoverished

☐ Laissez-faire

5.11 Fiedler identified that a leader could, at any one time, be people oriented or task oriented, but not both. The decision to be people or task oriented is based on three factors.

Which THREE of following according to Fiedler are the three factors which determine whether to be people or task oriented?

☐ Leader/member relations

☐ Group maintenance roles

☐ Task roles

☐ Concern for production

☐ Task structure

☐ Leader position power

5.12 Clarke and Pratt identified four different leadership styles which are dependent on the business's stage in its life cycle.

Which TWO of the following are leadership styles identified by Clarke and Pratt?

☐ Champion

☐ Early adopter

☐ Maturity remainer

☐ Star

☐ Tank commander

5.13 **Complete the definition of virtual teams below using the options provided:**

A virtual team is a team which is ⬚ ⬚ which makes use of ⬚ ⬚ to ⬚ team working.

Picklist:

geographically
information
dispersed
communications
support
technology
facilitate

5.14   John is the leader of a small team. He is regarded by his team as being a supportive leader, who is happy to provide team members with opportunities to develop their skills and careers. John avoids adopting a coercive leadership style.

Which style of leadership describes the approach taken by John?

○   Theory Y

○   Laissez-faire

○   Task oriented

○   Theory X

5.15   Distributive leadership is sometimes referred to as shared leadership, as leadership power does not reside solely in an appointed leader.

The creation of a distributive leadership approach can be encouraged by the presence of which THREE elements?

☐   Shared purpose

☐   Performance rewards

☐   Social support

☐   Appraisals

☐   Arbitration

☐   Voice

5.16   **Which TWO of the following factors might a leader adopt when creating an ethical culture?**

☐   Leading by example in the work environment

☐   Focusing solely on reducing costs and increasing sales

☐   Openly supporting good causes

☐   Only listening to concerns of key player stakeholders

☐   Adopting a coercive leadership style

5.17   **The work of which theorists is associated with the concept of situational leadership?**

○   Tannenbaum and Schmidt

○   Goold and Campbell

○   Hersey and Blanchard

○   Burns and Stalker

6 Managing performance

6.1 (1) The control environment is the embodiment of the workforce's approach to business, style and organisational policies.

(2) Control procedures are the mechanisms used by organisations to ensure control is maintained, they include: segregation of duties and authorisation limits.

Which of the following is correct?

○ Statement 1 is true

○ Statement 2 is true

○ Both of the statements are true

○ Neither of the statements are true

6.2 Trust between management and the workforce is an important factor in organisational control. Historically, organisations have tended to adopt formal mechanisms of control.

Formal mechanisms of control are most consistent with which school of management theory?

○ The human resources school

○ Systems theory

○ Contingency theory

○ The classical school

6.3 Performance appraisal can be remembered using the TARA acronym.

What does the 'T' in TARA stand for?

○ Timing

○ Targets

○ Training

○ Task

6.4 **Which of the following statements about staff appraisals are true?**

○ They do not provide a fair basis for remuneration

○ They are an entirely objective process for assessing staff performance

○ They enable succession planning

○ They are part of the disciplinary process

6.5 Fred feels that his manager Abi is picking on him for trivial things like an untidy desk and omitting to close a file drawer. Abi feels that Fred's presentation of accounts is not up to the standard expected of a qualified Chartered Global Management Accountant and has told him so. The situation in the office has deteriorated with Abi threatening disciplinary action and Fred threatening to invoke the company's grievance procedure.

Which THREE of the following would represent appropriate action by Fred and Abi respectively?

- ☐ Abi immediately threatening Fred with suspension
- ☐ Fred discussing his grievance with a staff representative
- ☐ Abi retracting her threat of disciplinary action
- ☐ Fred threatening to report Abi to the professional body for unprofessional conduct
- ☐ Abi reporting the situation to her superior
- ☐ Abi resigning her position

6.6 Management control takes place at a variety of levels including the strategic, tactical and operational levels.

J Company is currently reviewing its control systems and you are required to advise the project team on the appropriate level at which each of the following aspects of control should be set.

Match each of the control aspects listed below to the appropriate level in the control hierarchy:

Level in control hierarchy:	Aspects of control:
Strategic	▼
Tactical	▼
Operational	▼

Picklist:

Setting and reviewing the organisational structure
Computerisation of inventory control
Setting of the production budget

6.7 You have been asked to advise on the most appropriate form of control in the various departments of manufacturing Company A.

The manufacturing department involves the assembly and packing of toy cars. Employees are paid a basic salary plus a bonus based on the number of cars produced minus an amount for any rejects. There is little in the way of control from management as employees know the level of performance required to meet the targets set.

Employees in the wages department attend to all payroll related tasks and provide management with the necessary information for control of operations. Employees in the wages department are required to follow an impersonal system of rules and procedures.

The finance department is staffed by professional accountants. The culture of the finance department is based on shared values and standards where employees 'buy in' to the goals and expectations of Company A.

Indicate which form of management control is appropriate for the three departments:

Departments:	Manufacturing	Wages	Finance
Management control type:	▼	▼	▼

Picklist:

Bureaucratic
Personal
Output
Clan

6.8 **Which THREE of the following according to Armstrong are features of performance management?**

☐ Line management

☐ Human resources

☐ Appraisal

☐ Operational

☐ Specific

☐ Future-based

6.9 Mark is a manager who is keen to introduce a systematic approach to performance management to help support the development of the individuals in his team.

Using the options, below match the correct activity against the steps involved in performance management:

- Manage performance continually throughout the year
- From the business plan, identify requirements and competences required to carry it out
- Draw up a performance and development plan for each individual
- Draw up a performance agreement, defining the expectations of individuals in the team
- Performance review

Steps	Activity
Step 1	
Step 2	
Step 3	
Step 4	
Step 5	

6.10 Michael is the owner of Steel Co, a small manufacturer of steel rulers. Michael is actively involved in overseeing all activities undertaken at Steel Co and makes all major decisions affecting the company. Steel Co does not currently employ any managers or supervisors. Michael is regarded by many of the staff at Steel Co as a charismatic and personable leader, who regularly rewards staff for a job well done. Despite this, Michael is not afraid to punish workers that fail to perform.

Which type of control strategy is being used at Steel Co?

- ○ Output control
- ○ Bureaucratic control
- ○ Clan control
- ○ Personal centralised control

6.11 Samantha works for WSC Co, a graphic design company. The culture at WSC Co is based on the shared belief that all team members are equally valued and should be respected. The Managing Director of WSC Co is keen that all employees have a greater degree of freedom in choosing how best to complete their allocated tasks.

Which type of control strategy is being used at WSC Co?

- ○ Personal centralised control
- ○ Output control
- ○ Clan control
- ○ Bureaucratic control

6.12 Nicola is the Production Manager at TTRL Co. She has just been told by the Production Director that she has failed to achieve one of her customer focused performance targets for the last month. The performance target stipulates that TTRL Co should receive 10 or fewer customer complaints per month relating to output produced by the production department. Unfortunately, last month TTRL Co received 16 complaints. Nine of the customers complained that they had not received their order on time. Nicola feels that this is unfair as the production department had sent all orders through to the delivery department by the agreed date so that orders could be issued on time.

Which of the following BEST describes the failings of the performance target set for Nicola at TTRL Co?

○   Unrealistic

○   Unobservable

○   Uncoordinated

○   Uncontrollable

6.13 Gary, a Chartered Global Management Accountant (CGMA) working at Swain Co, has recently read an article which talked about the importance of co-ordination and alignment in the setting of organisational performance targets. The article highlighted that the alignment of performance targets throughout the organisation should lead to a flow-down or cascade of objectives.

Match the terms below to the correct level in the diagram to illustrate the cascade of objectives throughout an organisation:

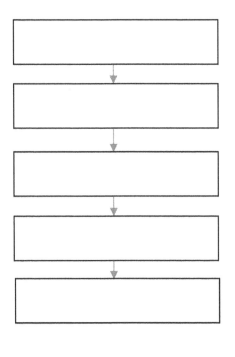
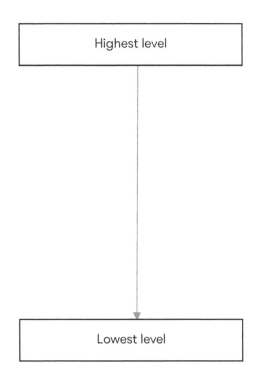

Picklist:

Tactical objectives
Mission
Individual performance targets and standards
Strategic objectives
Operational objectives

6.14   Darren is keen to give his staff greater freedom to decide how to undertake work-related tasks. He is particularly keen that his team start to use their initiative more, as he hopes that this will lead to more creative outputs. Darren is encouraging his team to make greater use of their skills, and has requested that team members approach him with suggestions about further training or development opportunities that they may be interested in.

Which of the following describes the approach that Darren is advocating?

- ○   Empowerment
- ○   Collaboration
- ○   Diversity
- ○   Alignment

6.15   Barry is about to undertake the appraisals of the staff members working in his team. Barry is hoping to use the appraisals as an opportunity to identify the individual career development needs of each team member. Barry is particularly keen to use the appraisals to predict the level and type of work that they will be capable of in the future.

What is the primary purpose of the appraisals that Barry is to undertake?

- ○   Reward review
- ○   Performance review
- ○   Potential review
- ○   Support review

6.16   Noel has been asked by his manager to prepare for his forthcoming appraisal by gathering feedback on his performance over the last year. Noel's manager has suggested that he approach colleagues, customers, and other key stakeholders to provide feedback on his performance.

Which type of appraisal approach is Noel's manager advocating?

- ○   Upward appraisal
- ○   360 degree feedback
- ○   180 degree feedback
- ○   Self-appraisal

6.17   Simon works in a call centre selling household insurances. He receives a fixed amount of $15 for every sale that he makes. Simon does not earn a basic salary in addition to any sales he makes.

Which type of rewards system describes the situation above?

- ○   Bonuses
- ○   Points scheme
- ○   Commission
- ○   Piecework

6.18 **Which of the following options is an example of an intrinsic reward resulting from work?**

○ Well-paid salary

○ Working conditions

○ Free health insurance

○ Status conveyed by position held

6.19 Terry has become aware that Matt, one of his employees, has recently started to arrive late for work and that the quality of his work has reduced considerably. Terry is about to go on annual leave for three weeks but intends to speak to Matt as soon as he arrives back at work.

In the context of best practice when handling disciplinary issues, which of the options will Terry have failed to consider by not dealing with Matt's behaviour at the current time?

○ Consistency

○ Impersonality

○ Privacy

○ The hot stove rule

6.20 **Which of the following is NOT a valid reason that an employer can use when making staff redundant?**

○ The employer has ceased to carry on business at all.

○ The employer has ceased to carry on business in the place where the employee was employed.

○ The employer discovered that an employee has joined a trade union.

○ The requirements of the business for employees to carry out work of a particular kind have ceased or diminished or are expected to.

6.21 'A type of dismissal that breaches an employee's contract of employment. An example would be failure to give the contractual period of notice.'

Which type of dismissal is being described in the statement above?

○ Redundancy

○ Unfair

○ Constructive

○ Wrongful

7 Coaching, mentoring and the work environment

7.1 Rosseau and Greller (1994) identified three types of psychological contract.

Which of the following was NOT one of types of psychological contract identified by Rosseau and Greller?

- ○ Coercive
- ○ Co-operative
- ○ Collaborative
- ○ Calculative

7.2 The use of coaching in the work environment has grown in popularity.

For coaching to be successful a series of steps need to be followed.

Using the options below match the activity against the steps involved in coaching:

Steps	Activity
Step 1	
Step 2	
Step 3	
Step 4	
Step 5	

Picklist:

Identify opportunities for broadening the trainee's knowledge and experience
Exchange feedback
Establish learning targets
Take into account the strengths and limitations of the trainee
Plan a systematic learning and development programme

7.3 **Which of the following statements is correct?**

- ○ Mentoring involves a trainee being put under the guidance of an experienced employee who shows the trainee how to perform tasks.
- ○ Mentoring covers a broader range of functions, and is not necessarily related to current job performance.
- ○ The mentor is always the trainee's immediate superior.
- ○ The mentee is the experienced individual who acts as the adviser to the mentor.

7.4 In Denison and Mishra's analysis, there are four possible cultures.

Match the culture beside the organisation to which it applies:

A large bread company exists in a stable environment, and its structure is well integrated. Management are preoccupied with efficiency with formal ways of behaviour.

[▼]

Hospitals are preoccupied with the sick; inevitably their values are patient orientated and staff's work has meaning and value.

[▼]

Picklist:

Consistency culture
Mission culture
Adaptability culture
Involvement culture

7.5 According to Schein, organisation culture exists at three different levels.

Which TWO of the following are included in the 'artefacts' level?

☐ Customs

☐ Dress codes

☐ Ceremonies

☐ Office layout

☐ Greeting styles

7.6 **Ouchi described the Theory J organisation (Japanese) as being characterised by which TWO of the following?**

☐ Long-term employment, with slow progressing managerial career paths

☐ Concern for employee focuses on work performance

☐ Explicit controls, formal measures

☐ Collective consensus decision-making processes

☐ Lay-offs are a common feature of the work environment

7.7 Foutts, an exclusive bank which only accepts the most affluent clients, has developed a culture which prides itself on the technical performance of its staff. Foutts is a very bureaucratic organisation and has a strong risk management focus.

Which of Deal and Kennedy's corporate cultures applies best to Foutts?

○ Process culture

○ Bet your company culture

○ Tough-guy macho culture

○ Work hard play hard culture

7.8 You are considering ways to make your business more successful and you have decided you want to reposition your organisation by offering unique levels of customer service in your industry. This change refers to the 'strategy' element of McKinsey's 7S model.

From the list below, identify the most appropriate element of McKinsey's 7S model and match them to the action to which it relates:

You might have to set up team-working in customer-facing units to increase responsiveness.	▼
You may need to train people in customer service skills.	▼
They will also need new procedures and IT systems for better access to customer data.	▼
Managers will have to adjust to empowering staff, and a new corporate image will be developed.	▼

Picklist:

Strategy
Structure
Staff
Skills
Systems
Style
Shared values

7.9 Research has indicated that workers in Country A display characteristics such as toughness and the desire for material wealth and possessions, while workers in Country B value personal relationships, belonging and the quality of life.

According to Hofstede's theory, these distinctions relate to which of the following cultural dimensions?

- ○ Power distance
- ○ Individualism and collectivism
- ○ Masculinity/femininity
- ○ Uncertainty avoidance

7.10 Bow-wing, an aircraft manufacturer, makes significant investments when undertaking projects to develop the latest commercial aircraft. The development of new aircraft can take many years before project completion.

Which of Deal and Kennedy's corporate cultures is Bow-wing likely to have?

- ○ Process culture
- ○ Bet your company culture
- ○ Tough-guy macho culture
- ○ Work hard play hard culture

7.11 **Which cultural type would BEST fit with a matrix structure?**

- ○ Person
- ○ Role
- ○ Power
- ○ Task

7.12 **Match Handy's Gods of Management beside the cultural organisational classification to which it applies:**

Task culture

Person culture

Role culture

Power culture

Picklist:

Zeus
Apollo
Athena
Dionysus

7.13 **Identify TWO benefits of health and safety controls from the following alternatives:**

- ☐ Employees breaking health and safety rules receive appropriate punishment.
- ☐ The company image is protected from a poor health and safety record.
- ☐ The morale of employees and others is improved.
- ☐ Health and safety controls save managers the job of monitoring potential safety hazards.
- ☐ The company's costs should increase.

7.14 The business case for encouraging diversity in the organisation's workforce is based on the recognition that, in order to compete successfully in the global economy, discrimination in any form could mean missing out on the recruitment of the most able talent.

Successful management of diversity therefore requires that an organisation takes specific measures to enable the optimum use of its staff.

Which TWO of the following are the MOST important measures?

- ☐ Supporting legislation against discrimination
- ☐ Encouraging flexibility in the treatment of all employees irrespective of their race, gender, age, sexual orientation, religion or politial affiliation
- ☐ Claiming the organisation is an equal opportunity employer in its mission statement
- ☐ Training managers in fair appraisal methods
- ☐ Operating from new premises

7.15 T has been newly appointed in the management accounts function at Q company.

T's first job is to meet with staff from various departments to discuss budgets and prepare revised forecasts.

T is unsure about the structure of the organisation and the responsibilities of the various staff within the departments.

T is therefore unsure where to start or who he should be speaking to.

Who would be best placed to advise T in relation to these concerns?

○ T's line manager

○ The Finance Director

○ T's mentor

○ T's junior assistant

7.16 **Which of the following describes the main feature of Adam's equity theory?**

○ The approach to the management of people at work based on equal access and fair treatment

○ The perception that workers have over their fairness of their treatment compared to others

○ The belief that the dimensions of individual difference on which organisations focus are crude

○ The employee has a fundamental duty of faithful service to their employer

---

7.17 Employers and employees have responsibilities in respect of health and safety.

Which of the following is a responsibility relating to employees?

○ To ensure that all plant and equipment is maintained to the necessary standard

○ To not interfere intentionally or recklessly with machinery or equipment

○ To introduce controls to reduce risks

○ To ensure that all work practices are safe

---

8 Managing relationships

8.1 **Which TWO of the following were identified by Steiner in terms of the basic ways in which groups function?**

☐ Additive

☐ Co-operative

☐ Distributive

☐ Conjunctive

☐ Collaborative

8.2   'A group created by managers to meet specific organisational objectives.'

Which type of group is being described above?

○   Informal group

○   Reference group

○   Autonomous working group

○   Formal group

8.3   Nisar has recently created a team to undertake a unique project at Sam Co to improve productivity across the business. Each team member was chosen on the basis of the specialist skills that they possess; as such every team member was drawn from different functional departments within Sam Co.

Which type of team has Nisar created?

○   Multi-skilled team

○   Productivity team

○   Multi-disciplinary team

○   Informal team

8.4   Vaill identified that high-performing teams have five common characteristics.

Which TWO of the following characteristics were identified by Vaill?

☐   Strong leadership

☐   Friendly team members

☐   Commitment

☐   Strong corporate culture

☐   Focus on innovation

8.5   **Which THREE of the following represent barriers to communication?**

☐   The choice of words provokes an emotional response

☐   Ensuring all elements of the communication fit

☐   The receiver filters out the elements that they do not want to deal with

☐   Limiting the encoding/decoding capabilities of the sender/receiver

☐   Physically nodding confirmation

☐   Responding to the points raised in a communication

8.6 Six factors are said to influence the choice of communication medium that should be used in any given situation.

Which THREE of the following are included in the six factors?

☐ Permanency

☐ Veracity

☐ Complexity

☐ Severity

☐ Urgency

☐ Transparency

8.7 There are many reasons why a message may not be communicated effectively.

For each of the situations below, identify the likely barrier which may prevent effective communication from occurring:

A phone conversation with a client is interrupted as a result of interference on the line.

Information relating to an organisational restructure is provided on a strictly 'need to know' basis.

The new CEO determines that email will now be used as the primary method of communication to ensure documentary evidence is in place should it be needed. This rule is to be applied to all messages from daily updates, to social events, to key operational messages.

Picklist:

Noise
Cultural values
Jargon
Priorities
Overload
Selective reporting
Timing
Distortion

8.8 **Which type of group is being described below?**

'A group that a person wants to join but is not currently a member of.'

○ Formal group

○ Informal group

○ Reference group

○ Autonomous working group

8.9 Team leader Arnica has given a team briefing stating the current situation and asking for suggestions to move the project on.

What stage is the team currently at?

○ Forming

○ Storming

○ Norming

○ Performing

8.10 A company has established a project team to design a new information system.

The team has had a few meetings to discuss how they are going to tackle the work and who would do what, but some early ideas have been unsuccessful.

Group members are still putting forward a number of very innovative ideas, but they often disagree strongly with each other.

The group members appear to be dividing into two camps each of which has an unofficial leader.

These two individuals agree about very little and appear to dislike each other.

According to Tuckman, which stage in group development has the project team reached?

○ Norming

○ Storming

○ Dorming

○ Forming

8.11 **Which of the following is a potential problem with individual performance rewards such as performance-related pay (PRP) when used as a motivator?**

○ It will always enhance team co-operation

○ Its relevance to business objectives

○ The fact that it does not relate to individuals' wage or salary grades

○ Its effect on team motivation

8.12 Grant is a member of a team. His colleagues in the team rely on him to read and check complex project documentation.

Grant has a keen eye for detail and often identifies minor details in documents that others miss but may be of significance.

Despite the diligent approach, Grant always meets his deadlines.

However, some of Grant's colleagues feel frustrated when he refuses to involve others.

He can hold up progress as he will not agree to the team signing off project documents until all of his concerns are fully discussed.

According to Belbin's team roles theory, Grant is an example of which of the following?

○ Implementer

○ Completer-finisher

○ Monitor-evaluator

○ Resource investigator

8.13 **Which of the following stakeholder groups is LEAST likely to be interested in the communications produced by the Chartered Global Management Accountant (CGMA) working in an organisation?**

○ Investors

○ Providers of finance

○ Customers

○ Tax authorities

8.14 Paul is a Chartered Global Management Accountant. He has provided you with a breakdown of the ways in which he has communicated throughout the course of the day.

Which TWO of the following are examples of non-verbal communication?

☐ Displaying encouraging facial expressions during a meeting

☐ Giving a presentation to the senior management team

☐ Participating in a series of conversations during a team meeting with the rest of the finance team

☐ Nodding during an interview for a new intern in the finance department

☐ Sending an email to the Finance Director

8.15 Participation can involve team members and make them feel committed to their task.

For participation in team environments to be effective, five Cs need to be present.

Which THREE of the following form part of the five Cs?

- ☐ Certainty
- ☐ Communication
- ☐ Collaboration
- ☐ Capability
- ☐ Clarity
- ☐ Commitment

8.16 The marketing manager at Swift Co, an online retailer has just been made aware of a fault with the company's major new product. The faulty product is only available for purchase via the Swift Co website. If consumers use the product there is a risk that they may suffer an injury. The marketing manager is keen to commence a product recall as soon as possible and wishes to alert as many consumers as can be reached about the potential danger.

Which of the following methods of communicating would be MOST appropriate to initially announce the product recall?

- ○ Sending a letter to Swift Co's customers
- ○ Posting an article on Swift Co's staff intranet page
- ○ Sending an email to all customers which have purchased the new product
- ○ Publishing an article in the weekend edition of three major newspapers

9 Negotiation and conflict management

9.1 J is preparing for a meeting with her line manager at which she hopes to negotiate a pay rise. She is gathering information to support her case and assist her negotiations.

Which TWO of the following types of information would you recommend would be suitable for inclusion in her case?

- ☐ Published statistics relating to market pay rates
- ☐ Examples of work she has performed in her previous job
- ☐ Spreadsheet showing J's salary in comparison with others in her department, which was prepared for J by her friend who works in management accounts
- ☐ A document which provides examples of poor work performance by J's manager
- ☐ Details of a client which represents a significant financial benefit to J's company that was obtained as a result of J's work

9.2 **Which THREE of the following are characteristics of successful negotiators as identified by Hunt?**

☐ They directly confront the opposition

☐ They consider a wide range of options

☐ They respond immediately with counter proposals

☐ They use emollient verbal techniques: 'Would it be helpful if we ...?'

☐ They summarise on behalf of all involved

☐ They take their time when speaking

9.3 **Which TWO of the below are the main elements involved in negotiation?**

☐ Purposeful persuasion

☐ Constructive compromise

☐ Conflict resolution

☐ Problem solving

☐ Distributive bargaining

9.4 There are five strategies for resolving conflict.

Match the correct labels in the boxes in the diagram using the list of words below:

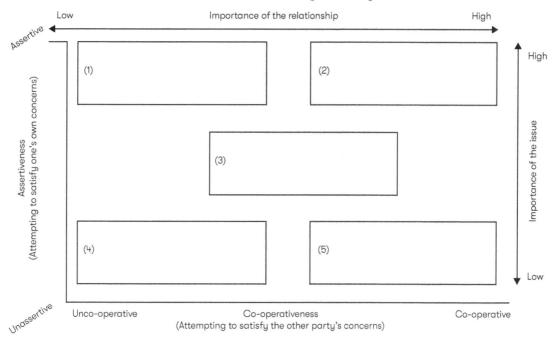

Picklist:

Forcing/competing
Accomodating
Avoiding
Collaborating
Compromising

9.5 **Aiming to find a 'win-win' solution is an example of which of the following?**

○ Distributive bargaining

○ Integrative bargaining

○ Purposeful persuasion

○ Conflict resolution

9.6 The trade union representing the workers of NickNack Company is threatening to take industrial action as a result of the decision made by the senior management to make changes to working practices without consultation.

What type of conflict does this represent?

○ Horizontal

○ Diagonal

○ Intergroup

○ Vertical

9.7 A new head of department is heading into her first negotiating role with a trade union. She has been offered a great deal of advice from colleagues, including the claim that each one of the following conflict handling strategies is the most likely to yield success.

Match the appropriate conflict handling strategy against each outcome:

Outcomes:	Conflict handling strategies:
Additional conflict will occur with damage to the organisation and to one or both parties.	▾
A win, win situation.	▾
Suppression of interests will result in one party losing out and difficulties may still remain.	▾
Lack of effort to deal with causes of the conflict will mean that conflict is likely to recur.	▾
Both parties lose out and there may be a better solution if an alternative approach was taken.	▾

Picklist:

Accommodation
Avoidance
Compromise
Competition
Collaboration

9.8   **Complete the definition of purposeful persuasion below using the options provided:**

Purposeful persuasion occurs where each [   ] attempts to [   ] the other to accept its case by [   ] arguments, backed by factual information and analysis.

Picklist:

negotiator
influence
force
pushing
persuade
party
marshalling

9.9   **Which THREE of the following make up the six principles of influence identified by Cialdini?**

☐   Reciprocity

☐   Authority

☐   Power

☐   Communication

☐   Social skills

☐   Scarcity

9.10   Conflict in organisations can be constructive or destructive.

Which of the following is an advantage of constructive conflict?

○   It can distract attention from the task

○   It encourages defensive behaviour

○   It can lead to the disintegration of a group

○   It can release hostile feelings

9.11   'A short-term approach to handling conflict commonly involves the threat of authority against those parties in conflict. It may involve denying the fact that a conflict has arisen, by downplaying the situation.'

Which strategy for managing conflict is being described above?

○   Conflict stimulation and orchestration

○   Conflict reduction

○   Conflict resolution

○   Conflict suppression

9.12 **The task of gathering information on the issues which will form the basis of a negotiation takes place at which stage of the negotiation process?**

- ○ Bargaining
- ○ Opening
- ○ Preparation
- ○ Closing

9.13 Callis Co has a functional structure with a number of specialist teams and departments all operating at different levels within the organisation.

Which of the following sources of conflict at Callis Co would be associated with vertical conflict?

- ○ Task interdependence between teams in different departments
- ○ Boundaries of authority between teams and departments
- ○ Cultural differences between different departments
- ○ Power and status of employees at different levels in the organisation

9.14 Members of the finance department at Daz Co are increasingly of the view that they are being neglected by senior management and other departments within the business. In response, the finance department has started to impose onerous rules and procedures on a number of teams and departments throughout the company in order to boost their own importance.

Which tactic of conflict is being described above?

- ○ Office politics
- ○ Distorting information
- ○ Fault-finding
- ○ Empire building

9.15 The board of directors at Jacob Co have agreed to increase the pay offer that they originally proposed to the company's staff representatives. The revised offer follows the rejection of the original offer by employees. The board of directors are hopeful that by making this concession that they will be able to reach a compromise agreement.

Which strategy for managing conflict BEST describes the situation at Jacob Co?

- ○ Conflict reduction
- ○ Conflict suppression
- ○ Conflict stimulation and orchestration
- ○ Conflict resolution

9.16 The task of fact finding about the opposing side's position in a negotiation takes place at which stage of the negotiation process?

○ Closing

○ Bargaining

○ Opening

○ Preparation

10 Introduction to project management

10.1 Darryl is a project team member working on an IT project. As this is Darryl's first involvement in project work, to help improve his understanding of project terminology he has just read an article about the importance of the project change management process. Darryl is recalling the information he just read to a colleague, but cannot remember the significance of recording project changes.

Which of the following BEST explains why project changes should be recorded as part of the project change management process?

○ Changes should be recorded so that appropriate disciplinary action can be taken against the individual that gave rise to the need for a project change.

○ Changes should be recorded to determine how much additional stress the project manager was required to handle.

○ Changes should be recorded so that an audit trail of the changes made exists so that this can be referred to at a later date and that lessons can be learned for the future.

○ Changes should be recorded so that senior management have an appreciation of the work undertaken by the project team.

10.2 **Which of the following is a feature of configuration management in project work?**

○ Considering whether the project can achieve the desired results in a cost-effective manner.

○ Tracking project changes and dealing with version control.

○ Completing the project within the agreed cost, on time and agreed scope.

○ Using quality control techniques to meet the end users' expectations.

10.3 Hannah is a newly qualified Chartered Global Management Accountant. She has just joined a project team at work and would like to gain a better understanding of project terminology.

Conformance management is primarily concerned with which of the following?

- ○ Inspection, quality control and quality assurance
- ○ Leadership, supply chain management, control, and problem-solving and decision-making
- ○ Initiation, planning, execution, control and closing
- ○ Transferring, avoiding, reducing, and absorbing risk

10.4 Libby is the project manager for an IT project which has the objective of improving the functionality of the company's website. This will involve designing a system which enhances the customer experience of navigating the website and simplifies the process for placing orders for the company's products – which are stationery items (paper clips, rulers etc) shaped like animals. The launch of the new website is time critical; customers need their tortoise-shaped drawing pins.

The project must be completed in three months' time but is experiencing significant slippage and is behind schedule. Which of the following things should Libby do to get back on track?

- ○ Maintain quality and reduce resources
- ○ Increase resources and increase quality
- ○ Reduce resources and increase quality
- ○ Increase resources and maintain quality

10.5 **According to the PRINCE2 methodology, which process ensures that all planned deliverables are completed as the project progresses?**

- ○ Initiation
- ○ Managing product delivery
- ○ Managing stage boundaries
- ○ Project assurance

10.6 **Which of the following provides a common understanding of a project for all its stakeholders by defining the project's overall boundaries?**

- ○ Project life cycle
- ○ Project milestones
- ○ Project initiation document
- ○ Project schedule

10.7 Which of the following terms is used in project management to assess how achievable various project options are?

   ○   Feasibility study

   ○   Risk analysis

   ○   Contingency study

   ○   Resource analysis

10.8 At what stage in the PMI's project management process is the scope of a project determined?

   ○   Planning

   ○   Initiation

   ○   Growth

   ○   Control

10.9 Which of the following correctly shows the three key constraints of projects which are commonly referred to as the 'iron triangle'?

   ○   People, finances, infrastructure

   ○   Risk, uncertainty, quality

   ○   Methodology, management, money

   ○   Scope, time, cost

10.10 What is the third stage in Gido and Clements's project life cycle?

   ○   Deliver the project

   ○   Execution

   ○   Implementation

   ○   Development of a solution

10.11 Cecil is the project manager overseeing a project, which had an original brief to introduce a new piece of payroll software. Over the last three months the board of directors have insisted that the project be extended to include the introduction of a piece of cutting-edge data analytics software to support the work of the marketing team. The board of directors are keen that the revised project should also include appointing three data scientists.

Which of the following options describes the problem outlined above?

   ○   Project slippage

   ○   Scope creep

   ○   Resource underutilisation

   ○   Risky shift

BPP
LEARNING
MEDIA

10.12   **Which quality assurance tool which requires a defect-free delivery of products and services 99.99997% of the time has been adapted for use in project management?**

○   PRINCE2

○   Project Management Body Of Knowledge (PMBOK)

○   Six Sigma

○   Microsoft Project

10.13   **Complete the definition of project management plan below using the options provided:**

A project management plan (also known as a project [   ] plan or simply project plan) outlines how the project will be planned, [   ] and implemented. It is used as a reference tool for both project [   ] and project [   ].

Picklist:

execution
control
implementation
quality
initiation
monitored
supervised

10.14   **What is the purpose of a project post-completion audit?**

○   To ensure that the project was delivered in full and signed-off as complete

○   To ensure that future projects benefit from any lessons learned from the way the project has been delivered

○   To ensure that all necessary documentation is completed

○   To ensure that the cost of the project was below the company's materiality level

10.15 Using the options provided below indicate whether the following descriptions are features of project work or business as usual operations:

Description	Features of project work or business as usual operations
Have a defined beginning and end	
Resources are used full-time	
Are often unique or only intended to be done once	
Often cut across organisational and functional lines	
Goals and deadlines tend to be more general	
Usually follows the organisational or functional structure	

Picklist:

Project work
Business as usual operations

10.16 Which of the following is NOT one of the four areas that the project manager should focus on during the implementation stage of a project?

- ○ Leadership
- ○ Resources
- ○ Control
- ○ Problem solving and decision making

10.17 Which of the following options shows in the correct order (starting from the first stage to the final stage) the 4Ds of Maylor's project methodology?

- ○ 1. Design 2. Define 3. Develop 4. Deliver
- ○ 1. Define 2. Design 3. Deliver 4. Develop
- ○ 1. Deliver 2. Develop 3. Design 4. Define
- ○ 1. Develop 2. Deliver 3. Define 4. Design

10.18 John is a project manager working at TEL Co. He is currently in the process of scheduling the various human resources needed to undertake a project to open a new office complex.

Which stage in Maylor's 4Ds project methodology has John reached?

- ○ Develop
- ○ Define
- ○ Design
- ○ Deliver

10.19 Which of the following is NOT one of the seven key themes in PRINCE2 which need to be considered if a project is to succeed?

    ○   Business case

    ○   Risk

    ○   Plans

    ○   Financial analysis

11 Project management tools and techniques

11.1 Which type of breakdown structure outlines the equipment needed to complete specific project tasks?

    ○   Statement of Work (SOWs)

    ○   Product Breakdown Structure (PBS)

    ○   Work Packages (WPs)

    ○   Cost Breakdown Structure (CBS)

11.2 What is the float time for a project activity if the earliest start time is day 5, the latest finish time is day 22, and the total time needed for the work is 14 days?

    ○   3 days

    ○   19 days

    ○   17 days

    ○   9 days

11.3 Bethan, a project manager, has identified a number of risks associated with her new project to open up a cat hotel. One of the risks has a high likelihood of happening, but will have a low impact on the project.

Which risk management strategy should be used here?

    ○   Transfer

    ○   Avoid

    ○   Reduce

    ○   Absorb

11.4 **Calculate the overall expected duration of the project:**

Activity	Preceding activity	Activity duration in weeks
A	–	8
B	–	10
C	–	6
D	A	8
E	B, C	9
F	C	14
G	D, E	14
H	F, G	6

- ○ 75 weeks
- ○ 39 weeks
- ○ 57 weeks
- ○ 25 weeks

11.5 **What is the duration of the critical path for this project?**

Activity	Immediately preceding activity	Duration (weeks)
A	–	5
B	–	4
C	A	2
D	B	1
E	B	5
F	B	5
G	C, D	4
H	F	3

- ○ 10 weeks
- ○ 11 weeks
- ○ 12 weeks
- ○ 13 weeks

11.6 **Which of the following can be used to manage project uncertainty, with specific reference to time?**

- ○ PERT
- ○ Financial feasibility
- ○ Economic feasibility
- ○ Work breakdown schedule

11.7 **Using the options provided match the term to the correct description:**

Term	Description
	Is used to analyse the interrelationship between project tasks
	Are a graphical representation of project activities
	Assists with uncertainty in project time planning
	Is an alternative approach to mitigating or managing risk which models possible future situations

Picklist:

Scenario planning
PERT
Network analysis
Gantt charts

11.8 **What is the float time for a project activity if the earliest start time is day 9, the latest finish time is day 43, and the total time needed for the work is 30 days?**

- ○ 13 days
- ○ 34 days
- ○ 21 days
- ○ 4 days

11.9 Deborah is managing a project which has been established to develop a new piece of payroll software at HTF Co.

Which of the following options is NOT an example of an external risk facing the software project at HTF Co?

- ○ Change in legislation governing the tax rules relating to the sale of new software
- ○ The launch by a competitor of their own software system
- ○ A decision by HTF Co's board to add additional features to the software being developed by Deborah's team
- ○ News that the national economy in HTF Co's home country is entering a recession

11.10 Using the options provided match the activities to the correct stages in the project risk management process:

Stage	Activities in the project risk management process
Stage 1	
Stage 2	
Stage 3	
Stage 4	
Stage 5	

Picklist:

Assess risks in terms of impact and probability
Plan and record risk management strategies
Identify risks and record risks in a risk register
Review and monitor the success of the risk management approach
Carry out risk management strategies as planned

11.11 Tim has been asked to manage a project to build a new bridge which stretches over the sea between two countries. Although somewhat larger, a similar bridge was constructed last year in a different part of the world.

What category of risk does the new technology fall into?

- ○ Uncertainty
- ○ Socially constructed risk
- ○ Quantifiable risk
- ○ Financial risk

11.12 Steve is the project manager overseeing the construction of a new office complex. He has classified the risk of the building collapsing partway through the build as having a low probability of occurring due to the relatively standard construction techniques being used, but is aware that this would have a significant impact on the success of the project if it did occur.

Which risk response strategy would be appropriate in managing the risk described above?

- ○ Absorb
- ○ Transfer
- ○ Reduce
- ○ Avoid

11.13 **Using the options provided match the activities to the corresponding step in the process of scenario planning:**

Step	Activities in the process of scenario planning
Step 1	
Step 2	
Step 3	
Step 4	
Step 5	
Step 6	

Picklist:

Identify the issues arising
Group mini-scenarios into two or three larger scenarios
Write up the scenarios in a format that is most suitable for the project manager using them
Bring drivers together into a viable framework
Prioritise 7–9 mini-scenarios
Decide on the drivers for change

11.14 **Which of the following is project management software unable to manage?**

○ Actual data to measure progress against the project plan

○ Creation of standard and tailored project progress reports

○ Automatic creation of Gantt charts

○ Human factors such as the motivation of the project team

11.15 **Tufte identified four ways in which data visualisation can support project managers. Which of the following is NOT one of the four ways?**

○ Enhance communication

○ Boost collaboration

○ Maintain central control

○ Improve clarity

11.16 David has been asked to manage a project to build the world's first flying car. This will require the use of radical new drone technology that is being developed specially for this project.

What category of risk does the new technology fall into?

○ Uncertainty

○ Quantifiable risk

○ Socially constructed risk

○ Financial risk

11.17 Farmer's supermarkets has a reputation for only selling high quality food products. The Procurement Director at Farmer's supermarkets has recently established a project team to explore increasing the range of food products offered. A large foreign supplier of fresh meat products has approached the project team. The supplier currently supplies a number of Farmer's' competitors and is well known for selling meat at very low prices. Members of the project team have raised concerns that the quality of the meat offered by the supplier is of a lower grade than Farmer's supermarkets' existing products. They have also raised concerns over the supplier's track record for animal welfare.

Which risk response strategy would be appropriate in managing the situation described above?

○ Absorb

○ Transfer

○ Reduce

○ Avoid

12 Project leadership

12.1 Ross is the project manager on a large construction project. It has come to his attention that two key project stakeholder groups are having a dispute over the use of project resources. Ross has contacted both groups with the intention of starting a conversation about how they can reach a common goal and overcome the current issues giving rise to conflict. Ross is keen to move the dispute away from solely focusing on issues of self-interest.

Which type of dispute management technique is Ross attempting to use?

○ Mediation

○ Negotiation

○ Compromise

○ Partnering

12.2 **Which of the following project stakeholders is the person who provides the resources for a project?**

○ Project sponsor

○ Project manager

○ Project owner

○ Project customer

12.3 **According to Tuckman, at what stage of the process of group formation is it when members begin to set agreed standards and allocate roles?**

○ Storming

○ Forming

○ Norming

○ Performing

BPP LEARNING MEDIA

12.4 Although there are numerous benefits of working as a team, there can be some negative effects too.

Which TWO of the following are the negative effects of team-working?

☐ The Abilene Paradox

☐ Synergy

☐ Group think

☐ Problem solving

☐ Creativity

12.5 A team is winding up a challenging project that it has been working on for some time. Next week, the same team will go on to a new project with quite different challenges.

Which stage of the group development model is this team likely to be going through?

○ Norming

○ Dorming

○ Adjourning

○ Performing

12.6 Team member Tom is one of those people who is dynamic and thrives on pressure. He tends to be the one who challenges and pushes other team members, sometimes annoying or upsetting them, but also getting the team past difficult periods.

Which of Belbin's team roles does Tom exercise?

○ Plant

○ Co-ordinator

○ Implementer

○ Shaper

12.7 **Which of the following principles of classical management is challenged by matrix management?**

○ Structuring the organisation on functional lines

○ Structuring the organisation on geographical lines

○ Unity of command

○ Decentralisation of decision making

12.8 **Which of the following is NOT an advantage of a matrix structure?**

○ Dual authority

○ Greater flexibility

○ Employee motivation

○ Improved communications

12.9 A large supermarket chain has purchased land for a new out-of-town shopping development in an area of recognised natural beauty. The organisation is now preparing plans for an infrastructure development (road access, parking, power) project.

Using Mendelow's power/interest matrix, which strategy would the project manager of the infrastructure development project use to manage a local nature appreciation group?

○ Consult and involve

○ Keep informed

○ Keep satisfied

○ Minimal effort

12.10 Mr Squirrel has built a new team to work on a project. He has evaluated the group according to Belbin's team roles and has identified that the group is unbalanced. The group is missing a number of important roles necessary to be effective. Mr Squirrel needs someone to control and organise the group's activities, and there is no one who is chasing and ensuring deadlines are met. The group is also missing someone to support other team members and diffuse potential conflict situations.

Using the options provided, match the correct team role to the descriptions:

Someone to control and organise the group's activities

Someone to chase and ensure deadlines are met

Someone to support other team members and diffuse potential conflict situations

Picklist:

Plant
Co-ordinator
Shaper
Monitor evaluator
Completer-finisher
Implementer
Team worker
Resource investigator

12.11 **To be successful in the management of change, a project manager will need which TWO of the following:**

☐ An ability to adopt an appropriate leadership style for managing change

☐ Making use of formal means only to communicate with project team members

☐ To be sensitive to the environmental and organisational contexts of the change

☐ Drive change entirely from the top

☐ To only focus on project stakeholders regarded as key players

12.12 Which **THREE** of the following are roles of the project manager?

☐   Co-ordinates project activities

☐   Approves the project plan

☐   Provides resources

☐   Provides leadership for the project team

☐   Responsible for successful delivery of project objectives

☐   Initiates the project

12.13 Judith is the project manager of a project at YUP Co which is aimed at introducing a new piece of integrated software. The software will be used by a number of different departments, and as such Judith has held a series of meetings between the departmental heads that will be affected by the introduction of the software. Judith has encountered a number of disagreements with the departmental heads about which department should have the new software installed first. Judith is finding that she has limited power to enforce the departments to work collaboratively.

The problems being experienced by Judith are a common problem with which type of project structure?

○   Functional structure

○   Lightweight matrix

○   Balanced model

○   Heavyweight matrix

12.14 Which of the following is a feature associated with the role of a project manager as opposed to an operational manager?

○   Possess specialist skills in particular areas

○   Have direct technical supervision responsibilities

○   Closely involved in technical tasks in a particular area

○   Generalists with wide-ranging backgrounds

12.15 Which of the following attributes will be the **LEAST** beneficial to an individual serving as a project manager?

○   Possess good problem-solving skills

○   Be inspiring to members of the project team

○   Be proactive at ensuring repetitive tasks are completed on an ongoing basis

○   Have good change management skills

12.16   Tim has been a member of a project team for the last three months. Over this time, Tim has observed that very often when it comes to making decisions the team tends to support the suggestions put forward by Vernon, who is a member of the project team. Vernon is well respected by other members of the team and is regarded as being highly competent.

Which of Steiner's four models of team dynamics illustrates the situation above?

○   Additive model

○   Conjunctive model

○   Disjunctive model

○   Complementary model

12.17   Clare is a project manager, she is currently trying to resolve a series of conflicts that have broken out between different project stakeholders. Clare is keen to adopt an approach which focuses on meeting the needs of the most powerful stakeholders. She also keen to meet the basic needs of those stakeholder groups regarded as being less important, with a view to keep them sufficiently happy in the short term.

Which of the following approaches to resolving conflict among project stakeholders describes the situation above?

○   Exercise of power

○   Sequential attention

○   Side payments

○   Satisficing

Answers to objective test questions

1 The ecosystems of organisations

1.1 The correct answer is: Contextualised interactions.

There are a number of factors driving **customer demand in the digital age, which include**:

Contextualised interactions – Customers demand products and services that are tailored to their needs.

Seamless experience across channels – Customers purchasing products and services online expect the process of researching, ordering, paying and taking receipt of their purchase to be seamless.

Transparency – Customers are increasingly protective over sharing their personal information with organisations when purchasing products and services. They expect organisations to look after the personal information or data they hold about them.

Peer-review and advocacy – Customers are more inclined to read product and service reviews left by previous purchasers/users of an organisation's products and services. This places an expectation on organisations to become proactive in managing their responses to customer communications and reviews, as bad reviews can have severe detrimental effects on reputations.

1.2 The correct answer is: Peer-review and advocacy.

There are a number of factors driving **customer demand in the digital age, which include**:

Peer-review and advocacy – Customers are more inclined to read product and service reviews left by previous purchasers and users of an organisation's products and services. This places an expectation on organisations to become proactive in managing their responses to customer communications and reviews, as bad reviews can have severe detrimental effects on reputations.

Contextualised interactions – Customers demand products and services that are tailored to their needs.

Seamless experience across channels – Customers purchasing products and services online expect the process of researching, ordering, paying and taking receipt of their purchase to be seamless.

Transparency – Customers are increasingly protective over sharing their personal information with organisations when purchasing products and services. They expect organisations to look after the personal information and data they hold about them.

1.3 The correct answer is: Brand atomisation.

Brand atomisation – Products and services need to be designed so that they can be more widely distributed and offered on multiple platforms.

Other approaches in keeping ahead of customer expectations include:

Design thinking – Organisations need to adjust their mindset from one of simply producing a single product or offering a single service to designing a broader range of experiences for the customer. To do this successfully, organisations need to be able to learn and adapt as the needs of their customers inevitably change.

Experiential pilots – Organisations need to become adept at monitoring how their customers behave so that they are better placed to understand their appreciation and openness to new experiences. Organisations need to be alert of the need to continuously innovate their offerings, and prototype new products and services so that they are better placed to understand customer reactions.

Prototyping – Getting products and services to market quickly is vitally important. Organisations need to be prepared to launch early generations of the products and services they provide (even if not fully ready) so that they can gain customer feedback and incorporate this into future versions.

1.4   The correct answers are:

- Innovators find 'back doors'
- Speed of change

The other options were distractors.

Traditional regulatory frameworks are being challenged by the emergence of ecosystems in a number of ways:

The **speed of change** in ecosystem environments caused by significant data sharing, constant innovation and collaboration presents regulators with challenges in protecting the privacy of consumers whose data may be used in ways not originally envisaged.

Innovators find 'back doors' in ecosystem environments and are therefore able to constantly challenge existing regulations. This is evident in the so-called 'gig economy' where employment legislation is being challenged by new start-ups keen to avoid recognising workers as employees. Classifying workers as sub-contractors allows firms to save on holiday and sick pay entitlements, and other employment costs.

Ecosystems continually evolve and as such regulators need to develop rules and regulations which are capable of containing undesirable patterns of behaviour beyond the here and now, and into the future.

Ecosystems are global and organisations operating within them are increasingly likely to transcend the legal frameworks in operation in one country. This is also true in respect of the diminishing boundaries between the laws governing physical products and services, and those which are provided digitally. Developing truly global regulations is a particular challenge.

1.5   The correct answers are:

Stakeholders are people, groups or organisations that can affect or be affected by the **actions** or **policies** of an organisation. Each stakeholder group has different **expectations** about what it wants, and therefore different **claims** upon the organisation

1.6   The correct answer is: The five forces which influence the state of competition in a given industry.

Porter's five forces model illustrates the state of competition in a given industry. Porter suggests that these forces collectively determine the profit potential of the industry as a whole. As such the five forces are not concerned with the forces affecting one particular business, nor are they concerned with the forces which make-up the substitutes in an industry. The power of substitutes is one of the five forces. The five competitive forces are not concerned with the state of competition in a market as such but the industry which serves a particular market.

1.7   The correct answer is: Threat of substitutes.

The threat of substitutes is characterised by the provision of a product or service by a party which operates in a different industry but which satisfies the same customer need. Company A and Company B both operate in different industries as one is a train service operator and the other is an airline, but both provide a service which involves transporting people between London and Paris.

1.8   The correct answer is:

Ecosystems comprise a **complex web** of **interdependent** enterprises and **relationships** aimed at creating and allocating business **value**

ANSWERS

1.9   The correct answer is: An enhanced level of co-ordination with formally or informally shared ideals, standards or goals.

The co-ordination, arrangement and management of complex environments is Davidson et al's definition of orchestration. Linkages across the ecosystem environment which connect data, information and knowledge is the definition of connections (being one of Davidson et al's three components that make up interactions in ecosystems). Speed and direction of exchanges of value among participants is the definition of the course of interactions (being one of Davison et al's other three components of ecosystem interactions).

1.10   The correct answer is: Digital business platform provider.

ABC Co provides participants, being buyers and sellers with a platform from which they can interact with one another. As ABC Co does not buy or sell goods itself, it cannot be a retailer. The term digital operating model provider is not a recognised role in the context of ecosystems. ABC Co is not an IT hardware provider as it only provides users of its site with access to a virtual marketplace.

1.11   The correct answer is: Marketing and sales.

Marketing and sales is a primary activity in the value chain model. The support activities consist of firm infrastructure, technology development, human resources management and procurement.

1.12   The correct answer is: Inbound logistics, operations, outbound logistics, marketing and sales, service.

When these activities combine they add value to the end customer, which is referred to as the margin in the value chain model.

1.13   The correct answer is: Everyone-to-everyone process of exchange.

Davidson et al define value creation in an ecosystem environment as involving all participants in an 'everyone-to-everyone process of exchange'. This contrasts with the traditional approach to value creation found in a traditional value network where value is created in a sequential order.

1.14   The correct answers are:

- Simple
- Open

Advances in technology are driving the creation of ecosystem environments which are connected, open, simple, intelligent, fast and scalable.

1.15   The correct answer is: Reach.

The other two features of participants, according to Davidson et al, are role and capability. Role is concerned with the part that the participant plays in the environment. Capability is concerned with the activities undertaken by the participant in the environment. Range is not one of the roles of an ecosystem participant.

1.16   The correct answer is: Course of interactions.

The other two features of interactions according to Davidson et al are rules and connections. Rules are concerned with governing the environment through informal or formal principles. Connections are the linkages across the ecosystem environment which connect data, information and knowledge. Transactions is not a participant interaction recognised by Davidson et al.

1.17   The correct answers are:

- Experience provider
- Process provider
- Platform provider

The fourth role according to Davidson et al is asset provider.

1.18   The correct answer is: Process provider.

Process providers manage the processes undertaken by participants in an ecosystem to improve efficiency. An asset provider manages the assets or activities that are critical to an ecosystem. An experience provider adds value to the customer by creating personalised 'customer centric' products and services. Value provider is not one of the roles of an ecosystem participant identified by Davidson et al.

1.19   The correct answer is: Experience provider.

An experience provider adds value to the customer by creating personalised 'customer centric' products and services. A platform provider creates an environment which enables ecosystems to function. An asset provider manages the assets or activities that are critical to an ecosystem. Process providers manage the processes undertaken by participants in an ecosystem to improve efficiency.

1.20   The correct answer is: Shark tank.

A shark tank ecosystem consists of participants that focus on creating value through innovation and differentiation. Low barriers to entry mean that the threat of new entrants is high. The lack of orchestration means that participants have to look after themselves as no one party is actively pulling together the activities of the different participants.

1.21   The correct answer is: Wolf pack.

The wolf pack ecosystem features low barriers to entry with a high degree of orchestration. The activities undertaken by participants tend to be fairly simple.

1.22   The correct answer is: High degree of complexity and tight orchestration.

A shark tank ecosystem has a low degree of complexity and loose orchestration.

A hornet's nest ecosystem has a high degree of complexity and loose orchestration.

A wolf pack ecosystem has a low degree of complexity and tight orchestration.

2   The elements of business models

2.1   The correct answers are:

A business model is concerned with how an organisation is **structured**, the **customers** and **markets** that it serves, the **products** and services that it provides, and how it creates **value** for stakeholders over time.

2.2   The correct answer is: Create value.

Create value is the second stage in CIMA's four stages; it follows on from the define value stage where the focus is upon determining the groups that an organisation aims to create value for.

2.3   The correct answer is: PESTEL.

Organisations can use PESTEL analysis as a framework for analysing opportunities and threats in the macro-environment. The macro-environment includes a broad range of factors which affect all businesses and is made up of political, economic, social, technological, environmental and legal factors.

Porter's five forces relate to the micro-environment and those factors that affect an organisation's ability to operate effectively in a given industry. Porter's value chain illustrates the activities undertaken by an organisation in creating value. Kaplan and Norton's balanced scorecard focuses on four perspectives in the process of value creation.

2.4 The correct answers are:
- Legal
- Social

The proposed introduction of new data protection regulations would form part of the legal section of the PESTEL analysis, as this is concerned with issues such as laws and regulations and any changes to them. Social factors cover issues such as demographics and changes in culture. It is evident that a cultural shift is taking place regarding the usage of personal data, as the general population is becoming increasingly concerned about data protection issues. You may have been tempted to select technological factors; however, this relates to changes in technology and the way in which it affects ways of working. You may have initially wanted to select political factors but, as well as not being an option, the legislation has already been introduced so there are no direct political issues.

2.5 The correct answer is: Economic.

Economic issues in PESTEL analysis include: the impact of the economic cycle; inflation; interest rates; tax rates; and foreign exchange rates.

2.6 The correct answer is: Volatile, uncertain, complex and ambiguous.

VUCA business environments are those which change rapidly.

2.7 The correct answer is: Internal business perspective.

The internal business perspective requires organisations to focus on those business processes that they must excel at to achieve their financial and customer objectives. The aim should be to improve internal processes and decision making.

2.8 The correct answers are:
- Power
- Urgency
- Legitimacy

Power is concerned with the degree of power that a stakeholder group has over others. Urgency refers to the extent that stakeholder demands require immediate action. Legitimacy is concerned with whether or not the actions of the stakeholder group are considered appropriate in terms of the values of the organisation.

2.9 The correct answer is: Keep satisfied stakeholder group.

Institutional shareholders are unlikely to be interested in the roll out of a new piece of payroll software at Swift plc, and can therefore be classified as having a low degree of interest. They do however hold a large degree of power over the affairs of Swift plc due to their role as institutional shareholders. As such the management team at Swift plc should aim to treat them as a keep satisfied stakeholder group.

2.10 The correct answers are:
- Partners
- Processes
- Resources

The other two main features specified by CIMA are activities and outputs. Stakeholders and relationships form part of the 'Partners' feature. Inputs would form part of the 'Resources' feature, being those items needed to provide the products or services to customers.

2.11 The correct answer is: As a threshold resource.

An industry-standard piece of IT hardware would represent a tangible threshold resource. A threshold resource is one which is needed to meet the customer's minimum requirements.

2.12   The correct answer is: An intangible threshold resource.

The right of an airline to book landing slots at an airport, when all competitors have the same right, represents an intangible threshold resource. In this example, as competitors in the ecosystem have access to the same resources, no lasting competitive advantage can be gained from possessing them alone.

2.13   The correct answer is: As an intangible unique resource.

The patent for the new medicine represents an intangible unique resource as it offers the company a competitive advantage that others cannot easily imitate or obtain as it alone holds the patent.

2.14   The correct answers are:

Organisations need to have in place **processes** to turn **resources** into **outputs,** as these are its products or services. Processes are effectively the steps that an organisation takes to meet its **objectives**.

2.15   The correct answer is: As a threshold competence.

This question focused on competences, being those processes and activities that the manufacturer undertakes to produce mobile phones with basic functionality. Therefore, this excluded the two resource-related options. A core competence provides an organisation with a competitive advantage which cannot easily be imitated; this option does not apply here as the manufacturer is only making basic devices. As such the correct answer is a threshold competence as this is concerned with the activities and processes needed to meet the customers' minimum requirements.

2.16   The correct answers are:

- Design
- Quality
- Price

The design, quality and price of an organisation's products, services or experience offerings are central to its ability to attract customers according to CIMA. The other three options were distractors.

2.17   The correct answer is: Psychographic.

Psychographic segmentation makes use of variables such as interests, activities, personality and opinions. It is commonly used in relation to consumer goods since they can be designed and promoted to appeal on the basis of such variables.

2.18   The correct answers are:

- Cost model
- Revenue model
- Distribution of surplus

The cost model is concerned with the costs involved in defining, creating and delivering value, as they have a bearing on the extent of the value that is captured. The revenue model is concerned with setting appropriate prices for products and services to ensure that sufficient value can be captured after all costs have been deducted. Distribution of surplus is based on the notion that when value is created it will be shared with others, while the organisation will also retain some of the surplus itself.

3   Digital disruption and digital business models

3.1   The correct answer is: Veracity.

Veracity is concerned with the truthfulness of captured data.

The other options were distractors.

3.2   The correct answer is: Blockchain.

FinTech, is having a major impact on the world of finance and is growing fast, with many predicting that it will mean extensive disruption to established businesses in this area.

Cryptocurrency is a digital currency, which uses internet technologies to facilitate transactions made online.

Digital assets are items which are not available in physical form. Examples of digital assets include: computer files such as PDFs and images; audio files such as MP3s; and video files.

3.3   The correct answer is: FinTech.

Financial technology, or FinTech, is having a major impact on the world of finance and is growing fast, with many predicting that it will mean extensive disruption to established businesses in this area. It has had a particular impact on the banking sector as peer-to-peer lenders have started to replace banks for lending and saving services.

3.4   The correct answer is: Cryptocurrency.

Cryptocurrencies are a form of digital currency which do not exist in physical form; Bitcoin and Ethereum are two of the best-known cryptocurrencies.

3.5   The correct answer is: Digital asset.

Digital assets are items which are not available in physical form. Examples of digital assets include: computer files such as PDFs and images; audio files such as MP3s; and video files.

3.6   The correct answer is: The internet of me.

When thinking about how to deal with digital disruption there are five trends according to the World Economic Forum (2016a) that business leaders are encouraged to focus on:

The internet of me – users must be placed at the centre of a personalised digital experience.

Outcome economy – customers are attracted to outcomes, not just products.

The Platform (r)evolution – the evolution of platforms is speeding up all of the time, offering opportunities for innovation and faster service delivery.

The intelligent enterprise – organisations should harness data to increase innovation and efficiency.

Workforce reimagined – as AI grows human resources should be deployed in different ways, not removed altogether.

3.7   The correct answer is: The Platform (r)evolution.

The Platform (r)evolution – the evolution of platforms is speeding up all of the time, offering opportunities for innovation and faster service delivery.

3.8   The correct answer is: Internet of Things.

The emergence of the so-called Internet of Things has resulted in sensors (such as RFID tags) and tracking devices being embedded and used in products and services. Some organisations have taken to using sensors to measure the efficiency of their operations as well. Automation is concerned with greater levels of robotic technologies, and is common in manufacturing environments. Artificial intelligence is concerned with the use of machines which are capable of thinking like human beings. Cloud computing is concerned with the use of cloud servers which enable users to save and access files remotely.

3.9   The correct answer is: Build strategy.

A build strategy involves an organisation developing its internal capabilities and infrastructures so that it can change the way it currently operates. Hiring tech savvy workers is central to this strategy.

3.10   The correct answer is: Partner strategy.

A partner strategy involves an established organisation (such as Zuma) working with a digital disruptor (Muzic Choice) to learn about the markets that it serves, and the products and services that it provides. This approach is appropriate for established businesses which are keen to discover more about emerging technologies used by other businesses, as they can avoid incurring the costs of acquiring the partner entity.

3.11   The correct answer is: Invest strategy.

The situation involving Small Co and Large plc is representative of an invest strategy, as it involves an entity (usually a larger entity) investing in a potentially interesting start-up. This provides the investing organisation with access to the skills and capabilities of the start-up without acquiring it. In this case Large plc has gained access to the skills of those technicians involved in developing software at Small Co. As is the case with Large plc and Small Co, investing organisations do not have control over the start-up.

3.12   The correct answer is: Incubate/accelerate strategy.

You may have been tempted to select the invest strategy option, given that Mac Dermot's had purchased a small number of shares in Eat Now; however, as Mac Dermot's board had announced plans to deploy its own internal capabilities in the form of a small team from its marketing department to assist with promoting the mobile app, this made it an incubate/accelerate strategy.

3.13   The correct answer is: Xtra-Frugal.

The Xtra-Frugal digital operating model requires the organisation to develop a less is more culture, and optimise internal processes. The formulation of a centralised organisational structure is a common feature of this.

3.14   The correct answers are:

* Formulate a centralised organisational structure
* Develop a strong engineer culture with a focus on automation
* Improve productivity and flexibility

The Skynet digital operating model makes use of machines, robotics and artificial intelligence. The hub and spoke organisational structure is a feature of the data-powered model. Developing an ecosystem environment is a feature of an Open and Liquid model. Empowering customer-facing staff is a feature of the customer-centric model.

3.15   The correct answer is: Open and Liquid.

The Open and Liquid digital operating model is outward looking and is focused on enhancing the organisation's offering to its customers by interacting with external participants. This is evident in the case of Willow as the company has developed a culture based on sharing information with the car rental company to benefit its own customers.

3.16   The correct answer is: Customer-centric.

The customer-centric digital operating model is focused on the customer. This is clearly the case at Nile plc given the company's customer-first ethos and the fact that all customer-facing staff are empowered to better meet the needs of its customers.

3.17   The correct answer is: Skynet.

The Skynet digital operating model makes use of machines, robots and artificial intelligence. Bell Co makes use of a basic artificial intelligence system through the use of the chatbot system which handles frequently asked questions. The use of the website, robotic machinery in the Manufacturing Department, and the focus on productivity among the management team all support the Skynet classification.

3.18   The correct answers are:

* Permit staff greater freedom to be creative in product development
* Encourage staff to challenge existing ways of working

Both of these approaches are mentioned by the World Economic Forum when attempting to foster a digital culture. It is likely that most staff at AMB Co will already use a computer as part of their day-to-day work; therefore this will not have any bearing on developing the company's culture. Also, there may be roles that do not require computer access (eg cleaning). Providing staff with an induction which focuses on AMB Co's origins will not foster a digital culture but instead reinforce existing ways of working. Appointing a new team leader to oversee the work of the admin team will not necessarily help to foster a digital culture.

3.19　The correct answers are:

- Become an employer of choice
- Harmonise environments

Becoming an employer of choice is Step 2 in the World Economic Forum's Seven Steps; harmonising environments is Step 6. Becoming an employer of choice means becoming a sufficiently attractive enough place that tech savvy individuals want to work for the organisation. Harmonising environments involves redesigning work spaces to encourage humans to work in closer proximity to automated machinery. Innovating on the periphery and copying successful digital firms are steps involved in disrupting existing business models, and are not included in the Seven Steps. Embracing the concept of scientific management is a method of micro-managing processes and is not directly relevant here.

3.20　The correct answer is: Integrate on-demand workforce.

Integrating on-demand workers is the seventh step in the World Economic Forum's steps of creating a digital workforce. This step involves organisations making use of on-demand workers (ie third party sub contractors) with relevant digital skills, which can be brought into an organisation as and when they are needed.

3.21　The correct answer is: A lack of technical knowledge among Toyz For You's management team about developing an online presence.

The lack of technical knowledge was the only internal factor listed as the others all related to external factors which might affect Toyz For You. Given that Toyz For You does not currently have an online presence and has operated physical shops for over 50 years this increases the likelihood that the company's management team will lack the technical knowledge to set up a website and social media presence.

3.22　The correct answer is: Hire digitally savvy individuals.

Hiring digitally savvy individuals is a feature of Step 2 (hire 'black ops' or 'hacking teams') in the process. Step 1 involves innovating on the periphery, and Step 3 involves copying successful firms such as Google.

3.23　The correct answer is: Automation.

The 'Quick' button represents the automation of a process which would have previously required customers to either physically go into a competitor's store or use the main River company website.

3.24　The correct answer is: The reduction in recruitment and associated costs.

The reduction in recruitment and associated costs is not a direct advantage of creating a digital workforce, ie directly related to the work that a digital workforce would perform. In fact, the costs associated with recruitment are likely to increase as new skills and experience are brought in. The other options listed were direct advantages of creating a digital workforce.

3.25　The correct answer is: Customer-centric.

The customer-centric digital operating model leads to the formation of decentralised organisational structure which supports the empowerment of staff.

4   Key concepts in management

4.1   The correct answer is: Awareness of the importance of group dynamics and worker attitudes as an influence on productivity.

Productivity and efficiency are not central concerns of human relations; rather, this could apply to the scientific management school.

Awareness of the variables affecting a manager is a contribution of the contingency school.

Proof of a link between job satisfaction, worker motivation and business success has not yet been provided by any school of management or motivation theory; apart from anything else, business success depends on factors other than the productivity of the workers.

4.2   The correct answer is: Inspirational.

Mintzberg grouped a manager's activities into the three roles of being interpersonal, informational and decisional. Inspirational is more akin to the interpersonal role as this requires the manager to act as a figurehead, and to lead and liaise.

4.3   The correct answers are:

- Set objectives for the organisation
- Organise the work

Drucker (1989) argued that organisational performance could be improved by aligning personal and departmental objectives with key business objectives.

The other options listed in the question were distractors.

4.4   The correct answers are:

- An airline
- A design agency

A sports team will need to work hard to foster team spirit at all times; the shamrock does not allow for this.

The management consultant and freelance doctor as sole traders will probably need to be all elements of the shamrock all of the time.

4.5   The correct answer is: Herzberg.

Fayol classified five functions of management. Drucker proposed the notion of management by objectives.

Maslow's work focused on a hierarchy of needs.

4.6   The correct answers is: There are differences of status, determined by people's greater expertise and experience.

In an organic organisation the business is its people, pay scales will be flexible and procedures are open to interpretation.

4.7   The correct answer is: The professional core.

'Peripheral group' is a distractor. Flexible labour force and the contractual fringe are used on an ad-hoc basis and are hired for a specific purpose so would not need to be multi-skilled.

4.8   The correct answers are:

- Planning
- Commanding
- Controlling

Orchestrating, arranging and communicating were all distractors.

4.9 The correct answer is: Weber.

Weber is associated with the study of bureaucracy, which also forms part of the classical school of management thinking.

Frederick W Taylor pioneered the scientific management movement in the US. Taylor was a very skilled engineer, and he took an engineering efficiency approach to management. Scientific management forms part of the classical school of management thinking.

Mayo's work is associated with the Hawthorne Studies, which identified that people are motivated by a variety of psychological needs, including social needs. Mayo's work forms part of the human relations school of management thinking.

Herzberg's work was concerned with motivator and hygiene factors in the workplace.

4.10 The correct answer is: Mintzberg's three managerial roles.

Mintzberg's three managerial roles consist of: interpersonal, informational, and decisional roles.

Interpersonal roles are based on the manager's formal authority: they include the roles of figurehead, leader and liaison. Informational roles are based on the manager's position in internal and external information networks: they include monitor, spokesperson and disseminator.

Decisional roles relate to the work of the manager's department: entrepreneur, disturbance-handler, resource allocator and negotiator.

4.11 The correct answers are:

At WPW there were small, integrated work groups consisting of a skilled man, his mate and one or two labourers. There was a high degree of autonomy at the work group level. The group was paid for its work as a group.

| Social systems |

WPW then introduced new technology creating a need for larger more specialise groups. A single cycle of mechanised production might extend over three shifts, each performing a separate process and made up of 10 to 20 men. Physical dispersion also greatly increased.

| Technical systems |

4.12 The correct answers is: High degree of task specialization.

This is a feature of the mechanistic organisational form.

4.13 The correct answers are:

- They are ideal for standardised, routine tasks.
- Some people are suited to the structured, predictable environments.

The fact that communication is only through suggested channels will most likely decrease the amount of suggestions made, and bureaucracies do not enhance creativity due to the level of control present. Decisions are made slowly.

4.14 The correct answers are:

- Unpleasant working conditions
- Below market rate salary
- High levels of supervision and tight control

Other hygiene factors concern policies and procedures and social interaction.

The other factors in the list are motivators.

4.15 The correct answer is: Referent.

Referent power is the power that a person has because they are well liked.

Coercive power is the power a person has to assign punishment.

Reward power is the power a person has to confer rewards.

Expert power is the power a person has who is perceived to have expert knowledge.

4.16   The correct answers are:

- Flexibility
- New technology
- Delayering

Centralisation, increasing middle management and top-down management are all things that would decrease empowerment.

4.17   The correct answer is: Staff authority.

Staff authority is the authority that a member of one department has to give specialist advice to members of another department, where there is no line authority.

4.18   The correct answers are:

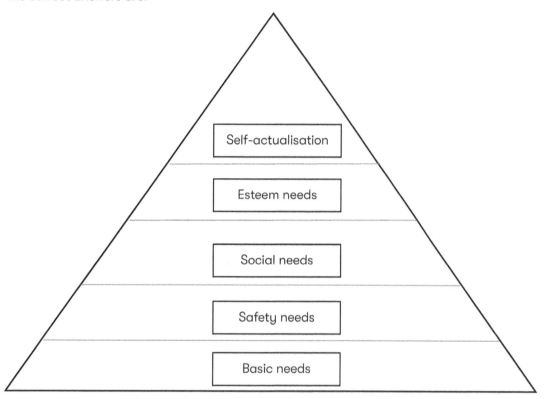

5   Key concepts in leadership

5.1   The correct answer is: Visionary.

This scenario will most likely require Dave to be effective in communicating the benefits of the new system in order to create inspiration among members of the finance team to get them to want to use the software. Visionary leadership is most appropriate during times of change; for example, when a new strategy needs to be implemented.

Being democratic is unlikely to be helpful as the opportunity for building consensus and permitting worker participation in the decision-making process will have limited effect as the type of software to be implemented has already been decided.

Adopting the pacesetting style requires workers that are self-driven, in this case as the members of the finance team are complacent this, approach would most likely not be appropriate.

The commanding style is most appropriate during times of crisis, which is clearly not the case in this scenario.

5.2　The correct answer is: Transformational.

Transformational leaders see their role as inspiring and motivating others to work at levels beyond mere compliance. Only transformational leadership is said to be able to change team/organisational cultures and create a new direction.

5.3　The correct answers are:

The leader has only superficial trust in subordinates, motivates by reward and, though sometimes involving others in problem solving, is basically paternalistic.

> Benevolent authoritative

The leader imposes decisions, never delegates, motivates by threat, has little communication with subordinates and does not encourage teamwork.

> Exploitative authoritative

The leader has confidence in subordinates, who are allowed to make decisions for themselves. Motivation is by reward for achieving goals set by participation, and there is a substantial amount of sharing of ideas, opinions and co-operation.

> Participative

The leader listens to subordinates but controls decision making, motivates by a level of involvement, and will use the ideas and suggestions of subordinates constructively.

> Consultative

5.4　The correct answers are:

I attend because it is expected. I either go along with the majority position or avoid expressing my views.

> 1,1 Impoverished

I try to come up with good ideas, and push for a decision as soon as I can get a majority behind me. I don't mind stepping on people if it helps making a sound decision.

> 9,1 Task Orientated

I like to be able to support what my boss wants and to recognise the merits of individual effort. When conflict rises, I do a good job of restoring harmony.

> 1,9 Country Club

5.5　The correct answers are:

A professional accountant should be straightforward and honest in all professional and business relationships.

> Integrity

A professional accountant should not allow bias, conflict of interest or undue influence of others to override professional or business judgements.

> Objectivity

A professional accountant has a continuing duty to maintain professional knowledge and skill and should act diligently and in accordance with applicable technical and professional standards when providing professional services.

> Professional competence and due care

A professional accountant should not disclose any information acquired as a result of professional and business relationships without proper and specific authority unless there is a legal or professional right or duty to disclose.

> Confidentiality

A professional accountant should comply with relevant laws and regulations, and should avoid any action that discredits the profession.

> Professional behaviour

5.6   The correct answers are:

Identifying those forces resisting change.

| Unfreeze |

Staff participation to help create the necessary 'buy in' to the new status quo.

| Change |

Gradually making the move towards its desired end state.

| Change |

A significant amount of management time will be spent reinforcing the adoption by staff of the new processes.

| Refreeze |

Strengthening the position of those forces driving the need for change.

| Unfreeze |

The new state being embedded.

| Refreeze |

5.7   The correct answer is: The ability to get others to follow willingly.

This is the role of a leader.

You may have been tempted by the option, 'the process of getting activities completed efficiently and effectively with and through other people'; this however is the definition of management. Challenging things taken for granted and translating the organisation's strategy to stakeholders are likely to be activities undertaken by a leader, but as the question asked for the best description of leadership these options were incorrect.

5.8   The correct answer is: Tells.

This is a tricky question. The characteristics of the project staff are such that a consultative or even democratic style might be recommended. However, the time and quality constraints mean that the project manager is likely to have to exercise firm control on occasion. This would probably be best done in a persuasive style. The conclusion is that the autocratic style will probably be of least use.

5.9   The correct answer is: Leaders are effective due to innate personal characteristics.

Trait theories assume that management skills (not leadership skills) can be taught but that leaders are effective due to the possession of innate personal traits or characteristics.

Style theory is concerned with the style that leaders use when interacting with others.

Distributive leadership is concerned with spreading the leadership role with others in a team.

5.10   The correct answers are:

- Authoritarian
- Democratic
- Laissez-faire

Exploitative authoritative is associated with the work of Likert. Theory X is one of the two approaches as proposed by McGregor. Impoverished is a leadership/management style proposed by Blake and Mouton.

5.11   The correct answers are:

- Leader/member relations
- Task structure
- Leader position power

Group maintenance and task roles are features of Adair's action-centred leadership theory.

Concern for production is one of the axes on Blake and Mouton's managerial grid model.

5.12   The correct answers are:

- Champion
- Tank commander

The Champion leadership style is commonly found in new entities where a leader is needed that will champion the cause of the business. As the business starts to grow the leader needs to adopt an approach that builds a supportive workforce, which is capable of exploiting future growth opportunities; this is the characteristic of the Tank commander style. Early adopter, star and maturity remainer were all distractors.

5.13   The correct answers are:

A virtual team is a team which is **geographically dispersed** which makes use of **communications technology** to **support** team working.

5.14   The correct answer is: Theory Y.

John would appear to be a Theory Y leader according to the work of McGregor.

A Theory X style leader according to McGregor assumes that staff have an inherent dislike of work and need to be coerced, directed and threatened to meet the organisation's objectives.

The laissez-faire style is associated with the work of Lewin et al. Laissez-faire leaders tend to not get involved with the teams that they lead and more or less allow their teams to run themselves. This clearly does not apply to the situation described.

Task oriented is one of the style classifications according to Blake and Mouton's managerial grid. The task-oriented leader sees people as a commodity to be directed or controlled like a machine. This does not apply to John.

5.15   The correct answers are:

- Shared purpose
- Social support
- Voice

A distributive leadership approach can be encouraged by the presence of three elements:

- All team members clearly understand the team's main objective (**shared purpose**).

- The degree of **social support** that team members provide each other

- The level of involvement team members have in deciding how the team meets its objectives (**voice**)

Performance rewards and appraisals were both distractors.

Arbitration is part of the role undertaken by ACAS, and was therefore incorrect.

5.16   The correct answers are:

- Leading by example in the work environment
- Openly supporting good causes

These two options embody doing the right thing.

Focusing solely on reducing costs and increasing sales heightens the risk that the leader may treat employees unfairly by placing unreasonable demands on them ie to work harder or longer hours unpaid. There is also the risk that the leader may expect staff to cut corners in terms of safety procedures to keep costs down or to act unethically to boost sales.

Only listening to key player stakeholders suggests that the legitimate claims of other groups will be ignored, which may result in them being treated in an unethical manner.

A coercive leadership style may result in the unfair treatment of staff, and is likely to be unethical.

5.17   The correct answer is: Hersey and Blanchard.

Hersey and Blanchard proposed the concept of situational leadership which focuses on the readiness of team members to perform a given task.

6   Managing performance

6.1   The correct answer: Statement 2 is true.

It is correct to state that control procedures are the mechanisms used by organisations to ensure control is maintained, which include: segregation of duties and authorisation limits.

Statement 1 is not true as the control environment is the embodiment of the **senior management's** approach to business, style and organisational policies, not that of the workforce.

6.2   The correct answer: The classical school.

The application of formal rules for the purposes of control are associated with the classical theories of management. These include the theories of Fayol, Taylor and Weber.

6.3   The correct answer: Targets.

The TARA acronym stands for:

Targets – Organisations must set targets which employees support and 'buy into'. The successful use of targets ultimately hinges on their perceived achievability (or not).

Actual results must be monitored – Managers should monitor the actual performance of employees during the review period and provide the subordinate with relevant feedback.

Review – Once the review period has ended the manager and employee should have a formal appraisal to evaluate the employee's performance. This will usually involve an evaluation of the employee's performance against pre-determined targets.

Action plan – New targets should be agreed between the manager and employee for the next review period.

6.4   The correct answers is: They enable succession planning.

Appraisals are the employee's chance to indicate where they would like to progress in the organisation so that this can be built in to their development plan, or they can be used by management to assess a candidate's readiness to move on.

Appraisals can provide a fair basis for remuneration, and can help to support cases where a pay rise may be in order, and because they are organisation wide, the HR Department can use them to ensure that staff at a particular grade have a similar skill set and are remunerated on that basis.

Because the appraisal is conducted by a person (or people), it is unlikely that it will be 100% objective. Appraisals do not form part of the disciplinary process.

6.5   The correct answers are:

- Fred discussing his grievance with a staff representative
- Abi retracting her threat of disciplinary action
- Abi reporting the situation to her superior

It does not sound as though Abi has grounds to suspend Fred, so this position may not be legally supportable. Likewise, it would not be appropriate for Fred to report Abi to the relevant professional body at this stage. Abi resigning her position was clearly a distractor.

6.6 The correct answers are:

Level in control hierarchy: Aspects of control:

Strategic | Setting and reviewing the organisational structure |

Tactical | Setting of the production budget |

Operational | Computerisation of inventory control |

At the highest level, the organisational structure is set and reviewed for appropriateness.

At the mid level of the organisation more detailed control is required to manage the strategic business units, such as the setting of budgets.

At the lowest level of the organisation very detailed controls should be in place, such as continual monitoring of inventory levels.

6.7 The correct answers are:

Departments:	Manufacturing	Wages	Finance
Management Control Type:	Output	Bureaucratic	Clan

This question tests your knowledge of control strategies. Output control refers to the control of the outcomes of processes, eg how much product is made; bureaucratic control is control through rules and procedures; clan control is control through corporate culture and shared behaviours. Personal control is a distractor, ie not a form of control. You may have confused the distractor with personal centralised control which is commonly found in owner-managed organisations.

6.8 The correct answers are:

- Line management
- Specific
- Future-based

Line management – A performance management system is primarily the concern, not of experts in the personnel/HR department, but of the managers responsible for driving the business.

Specific – As each organisation has unique issues to face, performance management systems cannot really be bought off the shelf.

Future-based – Performance management is forward-looking, based on the organisation's future needs and what the individual must do to satisfy them.

The other options were distractors.

6.9 The correct answers are:

Steps	Activity
Step 1	From the business plan, identify requirements and competences required to carry it out
Step 2	Draw up a performance agreement, defining the expectations of individuals in the team
Step 3	Draw up a performance and development plan for each individual
Step 4	Manage performance continually throughout the year
Step 5	Performance review

6.10 The correct answer is: Personal centralised control.

Personal centralised control is commonly found in smaller owner-managed businesses such as Steel Co. The fact that Michael makes all of the major decisions affecting the business, coupled to the fact that the company does not currently employ any managers or supervisors supports the personal centralised control classification. The use of rewards and punishment are also a key element of personal centralised control.

6.11 The correct answer is: Clan control.

Clan control is based on corporate culture. It depends on shared values and standards of behaviour within the organisation, and assumes that employees 'buy in' to the purpose, goals and expectations of the organisation. In such an environment individuals have a greater degree of freedom in choosing how best to complete their allocated tasks.

6.12 The correct answer is: Uncontrollable.

People should not be assessed according to factors which they cannot control. In essence, performance targets must be controllable. In this case, Nicola's performance is being measured against complaints resulting from failings in the delivery department, which, it would appear, have sent out the customer orders late. This is outside of Nicola's control. When the nine complaints are deducted from the 16 customer complaints received, this actually results in seven complaints. Therefore Nicola has actually met her target.

6.13 The correct answers are:

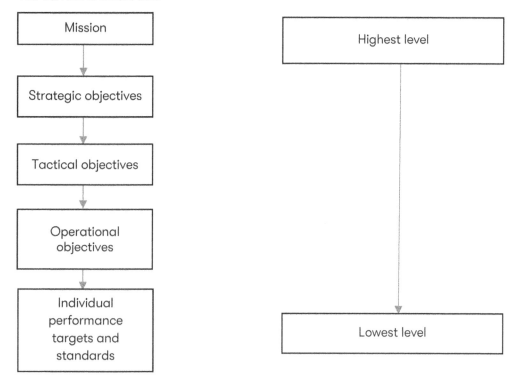

6.14 The correct answer is: Empowerment.

The situation described in the question relates to empowerment. Allowing workers to have the freedom to decide how to do the necessary work, using the skills they possess and acquiring new skills as necessary to be effective team members, is a central feature of empowerment.

6.15 The correct answer is: Potential review.

A potential review is an aid to planning career development and succession which attempts to predict the level and type of work that individuals will be capable of in the future.

Performance review and reward review are two further purposes of staff appraisals. Support review was a distractor; however it is likely that supporting team members would form part of a performance and potential review.

6.16   The correct answer is: 360 degree feedback.

A 360 degree approach aims to gather a rounded picture through feedback from groups including superiors, subordinates, colleagues, customers, and other key stakeholders.

6.17   The correct answer is: Piecework.

Piecework is a scheme whereby individuals receive a payment of a fixed amount per unit produced, or operation undertaken. This would apply to the situation involving Simon. You may have been tempted to go for commission. Sales commissions usually allow the individual making the sale of a good or service to earn a percentage based on the value of the item sold. Commissions such as this are usually earned in addition to a basic salary.

6.18   The correct answer is: Status conveyed by position held.

Intrinsic rewards are those which arise from the performance of the work itself. They are therefore psychological rather than material and relate to the concept of job satisfaction. Salary, working conditions and free health insurance are external to the job itself, and are therefore classified as extrinsic rewards.

6.19   The correct answer is: The hot stove rule.

The hot stove rule relates to immediacy. Immediacy means that after noticing an offence, ie an employee arriving late for work and producing poor quality work, the manager should take disciplinary action as speedily as possible, subject to investigations, while at the same time avoiding haste which may lead to unwarranted actions. Terry's decision to leave the matter for three weeks represents a failure to follow the hot stove rule.

6.20   The correct answer is: The employer discovered that an employee has joined a trade union.

Joining a trade union is not a valid rationale that an employer can give for making an employee redundant. Dismissal of this type would be deemed unfair.

6.21   The correct answer is: Wrongful.

Wrongful dismissal is dismissal that breaches the **contract of employment**. An example would be failure to give the contractual period of notice (assuming the circumstances did not justify summary dismissal).

Other types of dismissal include:

Constructive dismissal occurs when an employee resigns because their employer's conduct breaches their contract of employment, entitling the employee to resign and be treated as though they were in fact dismissed.

Unfair dismissal - The legal concept of unfair dismissal gives protection to the employee against **arbitrary** dismissal; that is, dismissal without good reason. The basic principle is that any dismissal is potentially unfair: once the employee has proved that they have been dismissed, the onus is on the employer to prove that the dismissal was fair.

Redundancy is defined as dismissal under the following circumstances:

- The employer has **ceased to carry on the business at all**
- The employer has **ceased to carry on business in the place** where the employee was employed
- The **requirements of the business for employees to carry out work of a particular kind have ceased** or diminished or are expected to.

7 Coaching, mentoring and the work environment

7.1 The correct answer is: Collaborative.

Rosseau and Greller identified the following three types of psychological contract:

- **Coercive** – This occurs where employees feel unfairly treated by their employer and do not regard the rewards received as adequate. Motivation is likely to be low in this type of contract.

- **Calculative** – This involves an employee voluntarily working in exchange for a reward. Motivation here can be increased if the rewards on offer are enhanced.

- **Co-operative** – Employees contribute greater levels of effort than is expected. They do this to help the organisation achieve its corporate objectives. Motivation and commitment are linked to the successful achievement of a task.

7.2 The correct answers are:

Steps	Activity
Step 1	Establish learning targets
Step 2	Plan a systematic learning and development programme
Step 3	Identify opportunities for broadening the trainee's knowledge and experience
Step 4	Take into account the strengths and limitations of the trainee
Step 5	Exchange feedback

7.3 The correct answer is: Mentoring covers a broader range of functions, and is not necessarily related to current job performance.

The other options were incorrect.

A trainee being put under the guidance of an experienced employee who shows the trainee how to perform tasks is the definition of coaching.

The mentor is not usually the trainee's immediate supervisor, and the mentor is the experienced individual who acts as the adviser to the mentee.

7.4 The correct answers are:

A large bread company exists in a stable environment, and its structure is well integrated. Management are preoccupied with efficiency with formal ways of behaviour.

> Consistency culture

Hospitals are preoccupied with the sick; inevitably their values are patient orientated and staff's work has meaning and value.

> Mission culture

Involvement culture satisfies the needs of its employees so that they give more to the organisation and the whole becomes more than just the sum of its parts.

Adaptability culture is where a company focuses on its environment and as a consequence, is continually changing.

7.5 The correct answers are:

- Dress codes
- Office layout

'Artefacts' are 'concrete expressions' and also include the above, but also literature and role models.

Customs relate to behaviours. Ceremonies and greeting styles relate to rituals.

BPP
LEARNING
MEDIA

7.6 The correct answers are:

- Long-term employment, with slow progressing managerial career paths
- Collective consensus decision-making processes

Theory J states that control is implicit rather than explicit, and that because employees stay with the company for such a long time, they become 'part of the family' so that concern for the employee's wellbeing stretches beyond the organisational boundary.

7.7 The correct answer is: Process culture.

A process culture focuses on managing risk and 'getting it right'. Do not be led astray by what you perceive a company's culture to be. In order to answer this question correctly you must focus on what the company is meant to do!

7.8 The correct answers are:

You might have to set up team-working in customer-facing units to increase responsiveness.	Structure
You may need to train people in customer service skills.	Skills
They will also need new procedures and IT systems for better access to customer data.	Systems
Managers will have to adjust to empowering staff, and a new corporate image will be developed.	Style

'Staff' refers to the number of people in the organisation and 'shared values' refers to the underlying beliefs and assumptions held by the organisation.

7.9 The correct answer is: Masculinity/femininity.

Power distance refers to the distribution of power. Individualism and collectivism refers to the extent to which people prefer to work in individualist or collectivist ways. Uncertainty avoidance is about the degree to which change is embraced.

7.10 The correct answer is: Bet your company culture.

This is because the company must make an extremely heavy resource commitment, usually for years, before any benefit of that hard work is seen. Failure to generate significant income after incurring such high costs would mean the end of the company.

7.11 The correct answer is: Task.

A task culture is focused on getting the job done in the most efficient way possible, and this usually requires the high degree of flexibility that a matrix structure provides.

7.12 The correct answers are:

Task culture	Athena
Person culture	Dionysus
Role culture	Apollo
Power culture	Zeus

7.13   The correct answers are:

- The company image is protected from a poor health and safety record.
- The morale of employees and others is improved.

Employees who break health and safety rules do not necessarily need 'punishment' but potentially re-education. The organisation may have guidelines on the consequences of rule breaking but this is not necessarily a 'control'.

Managers (and other employees) will still need to monitor for potential hazards no matter how many controls are in place. The option relating to the company's costs was a distractor.

7.14   The correct answers are:

- Encouraging flexibility in the treatment of all employees irrespective of their gender, race, age, disability, sexual orientation, religion or political affiliation
- Training managers in fair appraisal methods

Legislation must be followed regardless of whether it is 'supported' by the firm in question.

Just because an organisation claims something in its mission statement it does not necessarily mean that it practises what it preaches. Operating from new premises was clearly a distractor.

7.15   The correct answer is: T's mentor.

T's mentor would be ideally placed to guide T on these matters by providing overviews of the organisation and organisation charts and explaining the responsibilities of relevant members of staff.

7.16   The correct answer is: The perception that workers have over the fairness of their treatment compared to others.

Inequity can occur where individuals or groups perceive that their work efforts were the same as that of another person or group but they have not received the same level of reward: ie they have been paid less.

The approach to the management of people at work based on equal access and fair treatment relates to equal opportunities.

The belief that the dimensions of individual difference on which organisations focus are crude relates to the concept of diversity.

The employee has a fundamental duty of faithful service to their employer; this forms a key part of the employer-employee workplace relationship.

7.17   The correct answer is: To not interfere intentionally or recklessly with machinery or equipment.

The other options all related to the responsibilities of the employer.

8   Managing relationships

8.1   The correct answers are:

- Additive
- Conjunctive

The other options were distractors.

Steiner's theory consists of the:

- Additive model
- Conjunctive model
- Disjunctive model
- Complementary model

8.2 The correct answer is: Formal group.

Informal groups develop out of individual relationships and are based on shared interests.

Reference groups are those that a person wants to join but is not currently a member of.

Autonomous working groups are often used in improving productivity as individuals are put together to work in small cells or teams.

8.3 The correct answer is: Multi-disciplinary team.

A multi-disciplinary team contains people from different departments, pooling the skills of specialists.

A multi-skilled team contains people who themselves have more than one skill.

Productivity and informal teams were both distractors.

8.4 The correct answers are:

- Strong leadership
- Commitment

The five common characteristics identified by Vaill were:

- Clarity of purpose and near-term objectives
- Commitment
- Teamwork is focused on the task
- Strong leadership
- High levels of creativity and the generation of new ways of doing things

8.5 The correct answers are:

- The choice of words provokes an emotional response
- The receiver filters out the elements that they do not want to deal with
- Limiting the encoding/decoding capabilities of the sender/receiver

Where the choice of words provokes an emotional response, it may hinder the receiver from receiving the message clearly.

The other three responses will aid communication.

8.6 The correct answers are:

- Permanency – the need for a written record for legal evidence, confirmation of a transaction for future reference.

- Complexity – for example the need for a graphic illustration to explain concepts.

- Urgency – the speed of transition.

In addition, the choice of medium is also affected by the sensitivity/confidentiality of the message, the ease of dissemination and the cost effectiveness of the communication method.

8.7 The correct answers are:

A phone conversation with a client is interrupted as a result of interference on the line.

| Noise |

Information relating to an organisational restructure is provided on a strictly 'need to know' basis.

| Cultural values |

The new CEO determines that email will now be used as the primary method of communication to ensure documentary evidence is in place should it be needed. This rule is to be applied to all messages from daily updates, to social events, to key operational messages.

| Overload |

Noise is physical noise such as people talking around you or interference on a phone line.

Overload is getting too much information.

Cultural values refers to the way things are done in the organisation, eg whether there are open communication and knowledge sharing or whether people are only told what they need to know. A reluctance to give bad feedback/news may be a cultural factor.

Jargon is the use of specialist terminology that others may not understand.

Priorities refers to the business's priorities: the targets set by senior management.

Selective reporting is where subordinates only report key messages upwards to their superiors.

Timing is a problem where information has no immediate use so it is forgotten.

Distortion is where information is 'lost in translation': misinterpreted.

8.8   The correct answer is: Reference group.

Formal groups are created by managers to meet specific organisational objectives.

Informal groups develop out of individual relationships and are based on shared interests.

Autonomous working groups are used in improving productivity as individuals are put together to work in small cells or teams.

8.9   The correct answer is: Performing.

The team is executing its task and the team briefing is dealing with progress to date.

8.10   The correct answer is: Storming.

This is the storming stage, as identified by Tuckman. During this stage, conflict can be quite open. Objectives and procedures are challenged and risks are taken. However, there is a considerable amount of enthusiasm within the group and new ideas emerge. So too do political conflicts, as leadership of the group becomes an issue. This appears to be the situation described in the question.

8.11   The correct answer is: Its effect on team motivation.

Team members may work for individual rewards, rather than contributing to the group, especially since there is a problem offering rewards for less measurable criteria such as teamwork.

There is no guarantee that performance-related pay (PRP) will always lead to enhanced team co-operation.

You may have hesitated over the option about relating to wage and salary grades, but this is a benefit because PRP is a way of rewarding employees when there is no other way to do so (eg because they have reached the top of the salary/wage range their position is eligible for).

8.12   The correct answer is: Completer-finisher.

The key words in the question were 'keen eye for detail', 'always meets deadlines' and 'reluctant to involve others'. These phrases are typical characteristics of a completer-finisher.

8.13   The correct answer is: Customers.

Of the stakeholders listed it is likely that customers will be the least interested in the communications produced by the CGMA. Customers are more likely to be interested in communications published by the marketing and customer service teams, as they are likely to relate to the products and services offered by most organisations.

Investors will want to know how their investment is performing, and will spend time reviewing company financial statements. It is important that the CGMA accurately communicates the financial performance and position of the entity in a timely fashion, to support investors with investment decisions.

Providers of finance such as banks will likely require regular reports on key financial metrics, including a breakdown of the entities' accounts receivables and cash position, as these may form the basis for decisions concerning future financial support, eg extending bank loans.

Tax authorities will be interested in the entity's tax position.

8.14 The correct answers are:

- Displaying encouraging facial expressions during a meeting
- Nodding during an interview for a new intern in the finance department

Non-verbal communication is often called body language, consists of facial expressions, posture, proximity, gestures and non-verbal noises (grunts, yawns etc).

As giving a presentation and participating in conversations involve spoken forms of communication these do not represent non-verbal communications. You may have considered that sending an email to the finance director was a form of non-verbal communication as no physical words were spoken; however, it is important to realise that non-verbal communication relates to body language.

8.15 The correct answers are:

- Certainty
- Clarity
- Commitment

The 5Cs consist of the following:

- **Certainty** – Participation should be genuine.

- **Consistency** – Efforts to establish participation should be made consistently over a long period.

- **Clarity** – The purpose of participation is made quite clear.

- **Capacity** – The individual has the ability and information to participate effectively.

- **Commitment** – Support for participation.

8.16 The correct answer is: Sending an email to all customers which have purchased the new product.

To answer this question correctly it was important to pick up on the use of the words 'to initially announce the product recall'. Given the potential danger of the product the marketing manager wants to alert as many end consumers as quickly as possible. Therefore, in the short term an appropriate initial response would be to send an email to all customers which have purchased the new product. Swift Co would have the email addresses of all known customers that purchased the product as it is an online retailer. This approach should hopefully reach a sufficiently large enough audience as to raise awareness.

9 Negotiation and conflict management

9.1 The correct answers are:

- Published statistics relating to market pay rates

- Details of a client which represents a significant financial benefit to J's company, that was obtained as a result of J's work

Market rates of pay and details of J's own work and contribution are all relevant and should be used by J to help her secure a pay rise. However, highlighting examples of work performed in J's previous job will not be relevant to the current situation.

J should not have access to the salary levels of other members of staff and this should not, therefore, be used as part of her negotiations.

It is unclear how J would intend to use the evidence about her manager's poor work-performance, but this is not relevant to the current negotiation and this, nor any other form of bribery, should be used.

9.2   The correct answers are:

  •   They consider a wide range of options
  •   They use emollient verbal techniques: 'Would it be helpful if we ...?'
  •   They summarise on behalf of all involved

Hunt also identified the following characteristics of successful negotiators:

  •   They avoid direct confrontation.
  •   They hold back counter proposals rather than responding immediately.

9.3   The correct answers are:

  •   Purposeful persuasion
  •   Constructive compromise

The process of negotiation involves two main elements: purposeful persuasion and constructive compromise.

Conflict resolution and problem solving are examples of situations that negotiation can be applied to.

Distributive bargaining relates to negotiation.

9.4   The correct answers are:

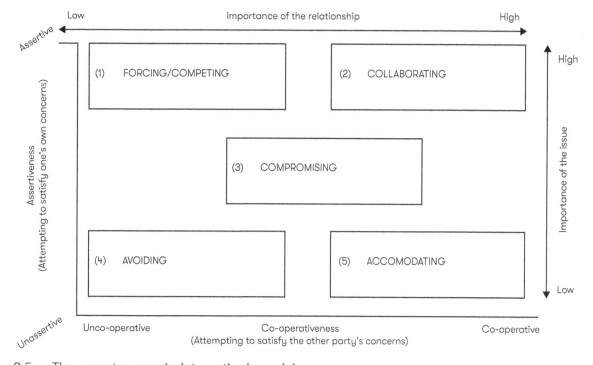

9.5   The correct answer is: Integrative bargaining.

Aiming to find a 'win-win' situation which fulfils the needs of all parties as far as possible is an example of the **integrative bargaining** approach to negotiation.

The distributive bargaining approach to negotiation is related to the distribution of finite resources.

Purposeful persuasion is where each party attempts to persuade the other to accept its case; conflict resolution aims to reduce resentment and preserve relationships.

9.6   The correct answer is: Vertical.

Vertical conflict is a result of a power imbalance so occurs between different levels of the organisation. Trade unions tend to get involved in this type of conflict most often.

Horizontal conflict occurs between different departments in the organisation.

Diagonal conflict is a combination of vertical and horizontal.

Intergroup is similar to horizontal in that it occurs between people at the same level of the organisation, but conflicting parties can be in the same department.

9.7   The correct answers are:

Outcomes:

Conflict handling strategies:

Additional conflict will occur with damage to the organisation and to one or both parties.

A win, win situation

Suppression of interests will result in one party losing out and difficulties may still remain.

Lack of effort to deal with causes of the conflict will mean that conflict is likely to recur.

Both parties lose out and there may be a better solution if an alternative approach was taken.

| Competition |
| Collaboration |
| Accommodation |
| Avoidance |
| Compromise |

9.8   The correct answers are:

Purposeful persuasion occurs where each **party** attempts to **persuade** the other to accept its case by **marshalling** arguments, backed by factual information and analysis.

9.9   The correct answers are:

- Reciprocity
- Authority
- Scarcity

Reciprocity is concerned with treating others in accordance with the treatment they themselves receive.

Human beings are more likely to be influenced by those people perceived as being in a position of authority.

A person's behaviour is influenced by the availability of a given item. In essence, if a particular item or proposal has limited availability ie it is scarce, it becomes more attractive.

The other options were all distractors.

9.10   The correct answer is: It can release hostile feelings.

The other options provided were features of destructive conflict.

9.11   The correct answer is: Conflict suppression.

Conflict stimulation and orchestration – This involves encouraging constructive conflict between individuals with the aim of getting people to generate ideas or to initiate change in the organisation.

Conflict reduction – This approach involves using strategies to bring conflicting parties towards shared objectives.

Conflict resolution – The focus of conflict resolution is to reach consensus among conflicting parties.

9.12　The correct answer is: Preparation.

Gathering information takes place in advance of a negotiation taking place. It forms an important part of the first stage in the negotiation process, which involves preparation.

9.13　The correct answer is: Power and status of employees at different levels in the organisation.

This is the only option that features employees operating at different levels in the organisation which is the key feature of vertical conflict. The other three options all related to conflict between teams and departments operating at the same level (horizontal conflict).

9.14　The correct answer is: Empire building.

The situation described in the question embodies the tactic of empire building.

Office politics might involve a manager seeking to bypass formal channels of communication and decision-making by establishing informal contacts and friendships with people in positions of importance.

Distorting information enables the group or manager presenting the information to get their way more easily.

Fault-finding involves deliberately finding problems in the work of other departments.

9.15　The correct answer is: Conflict reduction.

This approach involves using strategies to bring conflicting parties towards shared objectives. Compromise and concessions are commonly used techniques. Both of these are features of the situation at Jacob Co.

9.16　The correct answer is: Opening.

During the opening stage of the process each party should use this as an opportunity for fact finding, rather than point scoring. Negotiators should do this to gain a better understanding of the other party's position, including their strengths and their weaknesses.

10　Introduction to project management

10.1　The correct answer is: Changes should be recorded so that an audit trail of the changes made exists so that this can be referred to at a later date and that lessons can be learned for the future.

10.2　The correct answer is: Tracking project changes and dealing with version control.

Configuration management controls the processes by which projects evolve. It involves:

- Controlling project documentation to avoid version control issues
- Tracking changes to project documentation

Completing the project within the agreed cost, on time and agreed scope is a feature of the **iron (project) triangle**. Considering whether the project can achieve the desired results in a cost-effective manner is the main focus of the project **feasibility study. Conformance management** is connected to the issue of project quality. Conformance management systems are concerned with: inspection, quality control, and quality assurance.

10.3　The correct answer is: Inspection, quality control and quality assurance.

Conformance management is connected to the issue of project quality. Conformance management systems are concerned with: inspection, quality control, and quality assurance. These aim to ensure that the project adheres to the quality levels set out at the beginning of the project, by considering project performance against quality standards, with any deviations investigated and corrective measures implemented.

Leadership, supply chain management, control, and problem-solving and decision-making are the key areas that the project manager should focus on during the implementation stage of projects.

Initiation, planning, execution, control and closing are the stages involved in project management process according to the Project Management Institute.

Transferring, avoiding, reducing, and absorbing risk are four key quadrants from the risk assessment matrix.

10.4   The correct answer is: Increase resources and maintain quality.

Of course, the above is based on an ideal scenario where more resources are available. In real life this is unlikely to be the case.

It will be hard to maintain or increase quality if resources are reduced, and there is no need to increase quality.

10.5   The correct answer is: Managing stage boundaries.

This stage ensures that one stage is properly completed before the next one begins.

10.6   The correct answer is: Project initiation document.

A project initiation document states what is included and what is not within the scope of a project.

10.7   The correct answer is: Feasibility study.

This looks at whether a proposed project can achieve its objectives in a cost-effective manner.

10.8   The correct answer is: Initiation.

Project scope is all the things that have to be achieved if the project is to succeed. This should be done at the beginning of the process when the project is being initiated.

10.9   The correct answer is: Scope, time, cost.

Scope – this relates to all of the work that needs to be done and all of the deliverables that constitute the project's success. Scope is closely connected to the issue of quality.

Time – this concerns the agreed date for the delivery of the project.

Cost – this relates to authorised spend on the project.

10.10   The correct answer is: Implementation.

The four stages of the project life cycle are as follows:

Stage 1: Identification of a need

Stage 2: Development of a solution

Stage 3: Implementation

Stage 4: Completion

Deliver the project is the third stage in Maylor's 4Ds model. Execution is the third stage in the Project Management Institute's process.

10.11   The correct answer is: Scope creep.

Scope creep occurs where the scope of the project is changed without following a proper process. This would appear to be the case here as the objectives and aims of the project have expanded seemingly in response to the whims of the board of directors.

10.12   The correct answer is: Six Sigma.

Six Sigma is a rigorous operating methodology aimed at ensuring complete customer satisfaction by ingraining a culture of excellence. It requires the defect-free delivery of products or services 99.99997% of the time (ie as close to perfection as humanly possible).

10.13   The correct answer is:

A project management plan (also known as a project **quality** plan or simply project plan):

Outlines how the project will be planned, **monitored** and implemented. It is used as a reference tool for both project **execution** and project **control**.

10.14   The correct answer is: To ensure that future projects benefit from any lessons learned from the way the project has been delivered.

The post-completion audit takes place during the completion stage of the project life cycle. Ensuring that the project was delivered in full and signed-off as complete, and ensuring that all necessary documentation is completed both form part of the completion stage of the project life cycle.

Ensuring that the cost of the project was below the company's materiality level was a distractor.

10.15   The correct answers are:

Description	Features of project work or business as usual operations
Have a defined beginning and end	**Project work**
Resources are used full-time	**Business as usual operations**
Are often unique or only intended to be done once	**Project work**
Often cut across organisational and functional lines	**Project work**
Goals and deadlines tend to be more general	**Business as usual operations**
Usually follows the organisational or functional structure	**Business as usual operations**

10.16   The correct answer is: Resources.

The four areas that the project manager should focus on during the implementation stage are:

- Leadership
- Supply chain management
- Control
- Problem solving and decision making

The use of resources forms part of the focus of leadership and control.

10.17   The correct answer is: 1. Define 2. Design 3. Deliver 4. Develop

Define the project – Goals and objectives are set.

Design the project – Resources (finance, staff etc) are scheduled.

Deliver the project – Allocated resources are used to complete the tasks and progress is measured and corrective action taken where necessary.

Develop the process – The completed project is assessed as to whether it has met the objectives.

10.18   The correct answer is: Design.

The design stage involves scheduling resources including human resources.

BPP
LEARNING
MEDIA

10.19   The correct answer is: Financial analysis.

It is likely that the business case (being the reasoned account of why the project is needed) would incorporate some kind of financial analysis, but this is not recognised as a separate theme.

11   Project management tools and techniques

11.1   The correct answer is: Product Breakdown Structure (PBS)

The other breakdown structure approaches can be defined as follows:

Work Packages (WPs) – Outlines the work to be performed for each area (package) set out in the WBS.

Statement of Work (SOWs) – Sets out the deliverables from which the success of a project can be measured. It also specifies which member of the project team is responsible for delivering the work and by which point in time.

Product Breakdown Structure (PBS) – Outlines the equipment (products) needed to complete specific project tasks.

Cost Breakdown Structure (CBS) – Consists of cost-related information collected from the WBS, WP, SOW and PBS, in addition to capital and revenue elements. The CBS leads to the creation of the project budget.

11.2   The correct answer is: 3 days.

If the earliest start time is 5 days and the latest finish time is 22 days, you have 17 days in which to complete the project (22 – 5). If the work takes 14 days, that means you have 3 days spare (17 – 14).

11.3   The correct answer is: Reduce.

This will decrease the instances of the risk occurring. Even if the impact of the risk is not significant, it will consume resources if it keeps happening.

Transference is appropriate where a risk cannot be reduced and will have a significant impact on the project.

Avoidance is appropriate if Bethan can take steps to stop the risk from occurring at all.

Absorption is appropriate where a risk will only have a small impact on the business and cannot realistically be managed.

11.4   The correct answer is: The overall expected duration of the project is 39 weeks.

BEGH = 10 + 9 + 14 + 6 = 39 weeks

Activity-on-line style

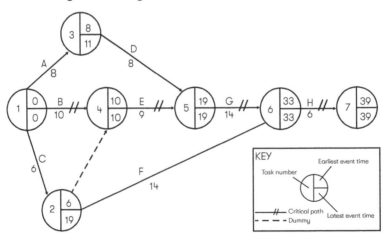

11.5   The correct answer is: 12 weeks are needed for the critical path B-F-H.

Activity-on-line style

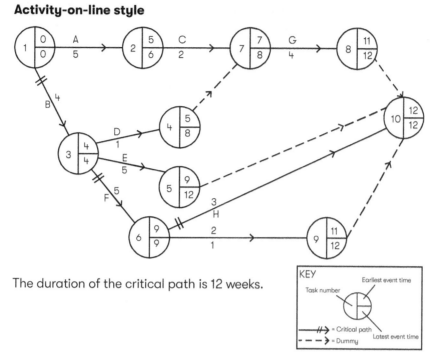

The duration of the critical path is 12 weeks.

11.6   The correct answers is: PERT.

PERT assesses how much work is done in comparison with how much work is remaining.

Financial and economic feasibility could reasonably be considered similar – concerning the profitability of the project rather than its timescales.

Work breakdown schedule is about the activities that need to take place during the project, not necessarily their duration.

11.7   The correct answers are:

Term	Description
Network analysis	Is used to analyse the interrelationship between project tasks
Gantt charts	Are a graphical representation of project activities
PERT	Assists with uncertainty in project time planning
Scenario planning	Is an alternative approach to mitigating or managing risk which models possible future situations

11.8   The correct answer is: 4 days.

If the earliest start time is 9 days and the latest finish time is 43 days, you have 34 days in which to complete the project (43 – 9). If the work takes 30 days, that means you have 4 days spare (34 – 30).

11.9   The correct answer is: A decision by HTF Co's board to add additional features to the software being developed by Deborah's team.

This is an internal risk factor as it has emerged from within HTF Co. The other risks were all external risks.

11.10 The correct answers are:

Stages	Activities in the project risk management process
Stage 1	Identify risks and record risks in a risk register
Stage 2	Assess risks in terms of impact and probability
Stage 3	Plan and record risk management strategies
Stage 4	Carry out risk management strategies as planned
Stage 5	Review and monitor the success of the risk management approach

11.11 The correct answer is: Quantifiable risk.

This is a quantifiable risk as its probability can be estimated by statistical analysis of past occurrences, ie the fact that a similar bridge was built last year.

11.12 The correct answer is: Transfer.

The significance of the building collapsing partway through the build coupled to the low likelihood of this occurring means that this risk would be best managed by transferring it by taking out a specialist insurance policy to cover such an event.

11.13 The correct answers are:

Step	Activities in the process of scenario planning
Step 1	Decide on the drivers for change
Step 2	Bring drivers together into a viable framework
Step 3	Prioritise 7–9 mini-scenarios
Step 4	Group mini-scenarios into two or three larger scenarios
Step 5	Write up the scenarios in a format that is most suitable for the project manager using them
Step 6	Identify the issues arising

11.14 The correct answer is: Human factors such as the motivation of the project team.

Project management software cannot record and manage human factors such as team motivation, even though these can have a profound effect on the project.

Project management software can manage the other options provided.

11.15 The correct answer is: Maintain central control.

The fourth way in which data visualisations support project managers concerns the interactivity that they provide.

11.16 The correct answer is: Uncertainty.

The new drone technology is radically new and not yet developed. As a result there is minimal historic data that could be used to calculate a meaningful probability. This means that the risk relates to uncertainty. There is no indication that the risk is socially constructed (ie not rationally assessed) or that there are risks around the financing of the project.

11.17   The correct answer is: Avoid.

Farmer's should avoid purchasing meat products from the foreign supplier. The decision to use the foreign supplier would clearly go against the company's commitment to selling high quality food products, as the supplier produces lower-grade meats. It seems likely that the project team's concerns regarding the supplier's record for animal welfare could reflect badly on Farmer's brand image should it decide to use the supplier.

12   Project leadership

12.1   The correct answer is: Partnering.

Partnering – Involves establishing communications between project stakeholders in conflict with a view to getting a conversation going about how they can reach a common goal, as opposed to focusing on issues of self-interest.

Other techniques include:

Mediation – Involves a third-party intervening to help project stakeholders in dispute resolve their differences.

Negotiation – Involves project stakeholders entering into discussions to resolve matters under dispute.

Compromise – This requires both project stakeholder groups in dispute to sacrifice something in order to overcome issues under dispute.

12.2   The correct answer is: Project sponsor.

The project sponsor provides and is accountable for the resources invested into a project and is responsible for the achievement of the project's business objectives.

12.3   The correct answer is: Norming.

At the norming stage there is agreement about work sharing and individual output.

Before the norming stage come the forming and storming stages. The former is characterised by unclear objectives and team members getting to know each other, as well as hesitance to put forward ideas because team members are unsure about others' reactions. The latter is characterised by conflict and possibly changes in previously agreed objectives.

Following the norming stage the members will enter the performing stage, where tasks are being performed competently and efficiently.

12.4   The correct answers are:

- The Abilene Paradox
- Group think

The other items are benefits of team working.

12.5   The correct answer is: Adjourning.

Adjourning is where the group sees itself as having fulfilled its purpose, and there is a process of disconnecting from the task and group because there will have to be a renegotiation of aims and roles for the new task.

Dorming is where a group grows complacent about performance. Norming is a much earlier stage in the cycle, where the group reaches agreement about work methods, roles and behaviours.

12.6   The correct answer is: Shaper.

The Shaper is the 'dynamo' of the team: one of the forms of leadership in Belbin's model.

12.7   The correct answer is: Unity of command.

Matrix organisation is based on dual command: the classical principle of unity of command is 'one person, one boss'.

12.8   The correct answer is: Dual authority.

Dual authority may lead to conflict between the managers involved.

The advantages of such a structure are:

- Greater flexibility
- Improved communications
- Employee motivation

12.9   The correct answer is: Keep informed.

Local nature appreciation groups would have high interest (due to potential environmental impacts) but relatively low power; because of their high interest, though, they might be able to band together or lobby to increase their power.

So a 'keep informed' strategy is appropriate to try to prevent them becoming a key player by campaigning to local government representatives or government bodies.

12.10   The correct answers are:

- **Co-ordinator** – controls and organises the group's activities
- **Completer-finisher** – chases and ensures deadlines are met
- **Team worker** – supports other team members, diffuses conflict

12.11   The correct answers are:

- An ability to adopt an appropriate leadership style for managing change
- To be sensitive to the environmental and organisational contexts of the change

By only using formal means of communication the project manager could make themselves less available and miss opportunities to demonstrate good management skills.

A change driven entirely from the top is lacking participation which is a powerful motivator.

Only focusing on those project stakeholders regarded as being key players is likely to be detrimental to the progression of the project, as a wide range of groups are likely to be affected by and to be able to affect the success of the project.

12.12   The correct answers are:

- Co-ordinates project activities
- Provides leadership for the project team
- Responsible for successful delivery of project objectives

The project plan is approved by the project sponsor who also provides the necessary resources. The project owner initiates the project.

12.13   The correct answer is: Lightweight matrix.

The project manager co-ordinates the project and chairs meetings between the departments involved. However, the project manager has limited power to enforce the commitment of departmental members. This would appear to be the case with the project at YUP Co.

The balanced model and heavyweight model are both types of project structure. The functional structure is a not a type of project structure, but is commonly used as part of business as usual operations.

12.14   The correct answer is: Generalists with wide-ranging backgrounds.

The other options all related to the role undertaken by operational managers.

12.15 The correct answer is: Be proactive at ensuring repetitive tasks are completed on an ongoing basis.

The need for good problem-solving skills is likely to be a necessity given the broad range of issues that arise during projects. Most projects require the project manager to interact with members of the project team, and as such the project manager will need to be inspirational and possess good change management skills. As such, ensuring that repetitive tasks are completed on an ongoing basis is likely to be the least beneficial attribute.

12.16 The correct answer is: Disjunctive model.

Disjunctive (collaboration) model is based on the idea that the most competent member is implemented. Effective for problem solving.

Additive model is based on the idea that each individual contributes independently of anyone else. Here output is inefficient.

Conjunctive (co-ordination) model involves high sequential dependence between members. Output is dependent on the weakest member.

Complementary model involves dividing the task into component parts with a different model for each task.

12.17 The correct answer is: Satisficing.

Satisficing – the strongest project stakeholders are satisfied; the rest are given enough to suffice.

Sequential attention – one objective is prioritised for a period before moving on to another one.

Side payments – disadvantaged project stakeholders are compensated.

Exercise of power – the use of force to resolve a deadlock.

Practice mock questions

Questions

1 There are 7 steps taken on a cyclical basis as stages in developing a Management by Objectives programme.

Match the following terms to the boxes, to show the stage that they relate to in developing a Management by Objectives programme:

(1)

(2)

(3)

(4)

(5)

(6)

(7)

Picklist:

Periodic review of performance

Define corporate objectives

Collaboratively define job tasks and responsibilities

Agree individual performance improvement plans

Agree and set specific task objectives

Establish system of monitoring, self-evaluation and review of performance against objectives

Agree and set specific key results

---

2 **Which of the following options BEST describes the approach taken by organisations towards competitors when operating in traditional markets?**

○ Sharing

○ Collaborative

○ Adversarial

○ Co-operative

---

3   According to psychological research on group development by Bruce Tuckman, at which stage in the process of group formation will members be wary about introducing new ideas?

○   The storming stage

○   The forming stage

○   The norming stage

○   The performing stage

4   Which TWO of the following statements about staff appraisal are true?

☐   They allow the employee and their assessor to discuss and agree on personal objectives.

☐   Reports on employees should be made out in writing and at annual intervals.

☐   They provide a system on which salary reviews and promotions can be based.

☐   They lead to improvements in performance.

☐   There should be no need to follow up after the interview has taken place.

5   Traditional business environments can be analysed using Porter's five forces model.

Which of the following is one of Porter's five forces?

○   Threat of new entrants

○   Threat of new stakeholders

○   Threat of new customers

○   Threat of new suppliers

6   Mr R is the project manager for an IT project which has the objective of improving the functionality of the payroll system to incorporate time and attendance reporting and hold complete human resource (HR) appraisal and training records for each employee. The launch of the new payroll system has been scheduled for two months' time. A new HR Director has just joined the company and at a recent review meeting it was evident to Mr R that the new HR Director did not feel the HR aspect of the system was fit for purpose.

Which of the following options should Mr R choose to ensure the project meets its objectives when delivered in two months' time?

○   Maintain quality and reduce resources

○   Increase resources and increase quality

○   Reduce resources and increase quality

○   Increase resources and maintain quality

7   According to the PRINCE2 methodology which process is undertaken to ensure that any given stage of the project remains on course?

○   Directing a project

○   Initiating a project

○   Controlling a stage

○   Managing stage boundaries

8   What term is used to describe stakeholder groups such as suppliers, customers and digital business platform providers that exist in ecosystem environments?

○   Competitors

○   Players

○   Participants

○   Facilitators

9   Consider a young Swedish engineering student taking a year out of university to gain work experience at a large car manufacturing plant in China.

    Which THREE of the following spheres of culture will the student be MOST influenced by?

☐   Ethnic group

☐   Gender

☐   Social class

☐   Profession

☐   Type of business

☐   Organisational

10 What is the float time for a project activity if the earliest start time is day 3, the latest finish time is day 21, and the total time needed for the work is 15 days?

○   18 days

○   3 days

○   6 days

○   24 days

11 Which **THREE** distinct components make up the interactions among participants in ecosystem environments according to Davidson et al?

☐ Rules

☐ Role

☐ Connections

☐ Reach

☐ Course of interactions

☐ Capability

---

12 Which **THREE** of the following represent barriers to communication?

☐ Encoding

☐ Informal communication

☐ Perceptual selection

☐ Jargon

☐ Selective reporting

☐ Decoding

---

13 Project Manager P has identified a number of risks associated with the project to upgrade and relaunch the company website. One of the risks relates to the capture of customer payment details, as it has just been discovered that the proposed software package does not meet the required banking security criteria.

Which risk management strategy should be used to manage the risk?

○ Transfer

○ Avoid

○ Reduce

○ Absorb

---

14   **Match the stage in the PMI project management process beside each of the activities to which it applies:**

Completing tasks according to the schedule

Ensuring the project meets the goals

Setting project goals and objectives

Recruiting the project manager

Measuring project progress

Picklist:

Initiation
Planning
Execution
Control
Project completion

---

15   **What name is given to the participant that formally organises the activities undertaken by other participants in an ecosystem environment?**

- ○   Collaborator
- ○   Orchestrator
- ○   Facilitator
- ○   Co-ordinator

---

16   **Which of the following is NOT a project constraint?**

- ○   Financial
- ○   Planning
- ○   Time
- ○   Quality

---

17   The Human Resources Director at RSJ Construction is disappointed with the results of a recent employee survey. The survey was conducted by a third party to ensure confidentiality, but only 150 of the 1,000 employees responded. Of those participating, high satisfaction scores were awarded for clarity of company policies and relationships with colleagues. Low satisfaction scores were awarded for quality of supervision and opportunities to advance in the company.

Which of the following should be the focus of the immediate corrective action by RSJ?

- ○   Introducing a new bonus scheme
- ○   Introducing a new leadership development programme
- ○   Introducing a new appraisal system
- ○   Introducing a training programme for existing managers

---

18   **Which of the following is a limitation of Gantt charts when used for more complex projects?**

○   Do not help estimate resources required

○   Do not display the time relationship between tasks

○   Do not indicate the need for resources to be co-ordinated

○   Do not indicate the time required to complete each task

19   Davidson et al identified four types of ecosystem depending on the extent of orchestration and the degree of complexity.

Which of the following are features of a hornet's nest ecosystem according to Davidson et al?

○   Low degree of complexity and tight orchestration

○   Low degree of complexity and loose orchestration

○   High degree of complexity and loose orchestration

○   High degree of complexity and tight orchestration

20   **Which aspect of project work is being described below?**

'Is a key point in the project life cycle that allows a review of project progress to determine whether to continue or terminate the project'.

○   Slippage

○   Control gate

○   Milestone

○   Scope creep

21   Control takes place at a variety of levels within an organisation.

Which of the following is a strategic-level control activity?

○   Setting organisational policies and procedures

○   Planning departmental budgets

○   Monitoring the performance of work teams

○   Processing invoices in the purchasing department

22   **Operational control is concerned with which TWO of the following?**

☐   Recruitment of factory managers

☐   Meeting with new suppliers

☐   Dealing with corporate governance issues

☐   Scheduling employee shifts

☐   Dealing with customer complaints

BPP
LEARNING
MEDIA

23 According to CIMA there are four stages in the process of value creation.

Which of the following is NOT one of the four stages involved in the process of value creation?

○ Capture value

○ Determine value

○ Deliver value

○ Create value

---

24 As the project has progressed, friction between team members has meant that two operational managers have gone back to their business roles and they have been replaced with two new team members. Mr A is a marketing analyst who is very focused on generating new ideas, while Mr B is painstakingly conscientious and delivers detailed solutions of high quality.

Using the list of options, match the relevant team roles that the new team members fulfil in the boxes below:

Mr A [　　　　　　　　　　　▼]

Mr B [　　　　　　　　　　　▼]

Picklist:

Plant
Monitor evaluator
Completer-finisher
Specialist
Implementer

---

25 Conflict can occur at many different levels in an organisation.

Determine which of the following causes of conflict will result in horizontal conflict, and which will result in vertical conflict:

		Horizontal	Vertical
(a)	Use of an integrated computer system	☐	☐
(b)	Operating separate bonus schemes for the sales force administrative staff and management	☐	☐
(c)	Increase in staff union membership	☐	☐
(d)	Reduction in headcount across the organisation	☐	☐
(e)	Staff managers encroaching on the roles of line managers	☐	☐

---

26 **What term is used to describe the value which is captured by a participant operating in an ecosystem?**

○ Residual value

○ Profit

○ Contribution

○ Value added

27 Oaktree Furniture Co has operated successfully for 30 years, with a skilled and stable sales force. Recently the company performance has begun to suffer and the sales force is being asked to explain the drop in sales and the logic behind their current strategy. At the recent team meeting, none of the sales force was prepared to justify the strategy, individually saying they did not believe in it even though nobody opposed the strategy when it was introduced.

What type of group problem is the sales force team experiencing?

○ Risky shift

○ Conformity

○ The Abilene Paradox

○ Groupthink

28 An organic ready-meal manufacturer has developed an exclusive range of meals for a national supermarket chain. A consumer has allegedly found some glass in one of the meals and has gone straight to the media about the poor quality of the supermarket's own brand. The supermarket has initiated legal proceedings against the manufacturer due to loss of reputation. The manufacturer's legal counsel has advised that they accept responsibility and agree an out-of-court settlement.

Which type of conflict-handling strategy is being recommended?

○ Avoiding

○ Accommodating

○ Competing

○ Compromising

29 **Which of the following is NOT a cultural element identified by McKinsey's 7S model?**

○ Style

○ Skill

○ Salary

○ System

30   The Chartered Global Management Accountant of a small retail chain has identified a number of areas for potential cost saving across the company's network of stores. He has highlighted this to the Supply Chain Director and requested a meeting to discuss this further.

What type of communication channel is the Chartered Global Management Accountant using?

○   Horizontal

○   Diagonal

○   Vertical

○   Intergroup

31   CIMA highlights that the process of defining value is an iterative process that involves four key steps.

Which of the following correctly shows the running order of the four steps?

○   1. Identification of the needs of the highest priority stakeholders, 2. Formulation of value propositions, 3. Ranking and prioritisation, 4. Identification of relevant stakeholders

○   1. Ranking and prioritisation, 2. Identification of relevant stakeholders, 3. Formulation of value propositions, 4. Identification of the needs of the highest priority stakeholders

○   1. Identification of relevant stakeholders, 2. Ranking and prioritisation, 3. Identification of the needs of the highest priority stakeholders, 4. Formulation of value propositions

○   1. Formulation of value propositions, 2. Identification of the needs of the highest priority stakeholders, 3. Identification of relevant stakeholders, 4. Ranking and prioritisation

32   **Using the words from the list below complete the sentences.**

Persuasion [   ] influence as it is always of a direct and [   ] nature. Persuasion is aligned to a particular objective which can only be achieved by [   ] the support of others. Persuasion is not the same as [   ] a person to do something, as it focuses on reaching agreement.

Picklist:

commanding
is similar to
deliberate
requesting
differs to
thoughtless
gaining

33   A new pricing model is being introduced at ABC Co as part of a business project. ABC Co's year end is in one month's time. At a recent project review meeting the project manager identified that the project had slipped behind schedule and that the new pricing structures would not be ready for release by the start of the new financial year.

Which option should the project manager use to deal with the slippage?

○   Do nothing

○   Add resource

○   Reschedule

○   Change the specification

34   A common failure of project implementation is the resistance to change among the existing workforce.

Which of the following is NOT usually a reason for resistance?

○   Introduction of new technology

○   Loss of autonomy

○   Rapid change

○   Structured training programmes

35   The IT Director has worked for the organisation for 20 years and is known to be a fair manager, ensuring his staff are rewarded with performance-related pay rises each year. A new Marketing Director has recently been appointed to the board and the IT Director has noticed the immediate impact the new director has had, with staff at all levels across the organisation readily doing additional pieces of work for him.

Which type of power is it likely that the Marketing Director is utilising that the IT Director does not have?

○   Reward

○   Legitimate

○   Expert

○   Referent

36   The Managing Director of a diamond mining company has recently read an article about the different types of resources that exist. She would like to gain a better understanding of how the company's diamond mines would be classified.

How would the company's diamond mines be classified?

○   As a core resource

○   As a tangible unique resource

○   As a threshold resource

○   As a key resource

BPP
LEARNING
MEDIA

37 **Which of the following is NOT an advantage of written forms of communication?**

○ Focus on personal interactions and relationship building

○ Provide subsequent reference for information and agreements

○ Provide legally acceptable evidence

○ Focus attention of sender and receiver

38 Sandeep has just joined the finance team of Iceberg City, a new restaurant chain based in city centres across the county. Following a rigorous interview and selection process, she felt she had a good idea of the organisational culture before she joined. However, by the end of her first month she has identified several aspects that she was not previously aware of.

Which TWO of the following would Sandeep MOST likely have been aware of before joining the company?

☐ The company's code of ethics available on Iceberg City's website

☐ The company's statement of values and beliefs available on Iceberg City's social media page

☐ Employee attitudes

☐ Departmental structure

☐ Informal employee networks

39 Age, religion, income, occupation and education are variables which can be used in the process of customer segmentation.

Which type of customer segmentation do the variables specified above relate to?

○ Behavioural

○ Psychographic

○ Socio-demographic

○ Geographic

40 **Using the options listed below, match the level of assertiveness with the importance of the relationship to identify the conflict-handling strategies:**

Conflict handling strategies	Level of assertiveness and importance of the relationship
[▼]	High: Assertiveness/Low: Importance placed on the relationship
[▼]	Low: Assetiveness/Low: Importance placed on the relationship
[▼]	High: Assertiveness/High: Importance placed on the relationship

Picklist:

Competing
Avoiding
Collaborating

41   Sally is the project manager at an IT consultancy. Due to the high performance of the team she leads, her team has been kept together for several years, outperforming expectations on each project they undertake. However, the latest project has run into several serious problems, and the customer will not sign off on completion as they are unhappy with the solution that has been implemented and feel a better solution could have been found.

What type of group problem is Sally's team experiencing?

○   Risky shift

○   Conformity

○   The Abilene Paradox

○   Groupthink

---

42   Mendelow's power-interest matrix can be used in the process of stakeholder analysis.

Using Mendelow's power-interest matrix how should a high interest, low power stakeholder group be treated?

○   Minimal effort stakeholder group

○   Keep satisfied stakeholder group

○   Keep informed stakeholder group

○   Key player stakeholder group

---

43   Team members should be selected for their potential to contribute to getting things done and establishing good working relationships.

This may include which TWO of the following?

☐   Specialist skills

☐   Interesting hobbies

☐   High academic achievement

☐   Age

☐   Power in the wider organisation

---

44   Mary is the project manager for the implementation of a new customer relationship management system. In preparation for her project status review meeting with the project sponsor, she has been reviewing the tasks completed in relation to the schedule, and allocating resource to the next set of tasks to be achieved.

Which stage of the project life cycle has the project reached?

○   Identification of a need

○   Development of a solution

○   Implementation

○   Completion

---

45   The World Economic Forum identified different strategies that organisations can adopt when creating disruptive business models.

Using the options listed below, match the correct labels against the descriptions to show the strategies that can be used in creating disruptive business models:

A strategy which involves an organisation developing its internal capabilities and infrastructures so that it can change the way it currently operates

[▼]

A strategy which involves an established organisation working with a digital disruptor to learn about the markets that it serves, and the products and services that it provides

[▼]

A strategy which involves an established organisation acquiring a digital start-up business. Acquiring a digital start-up enables the organisation to gain access to the innovative technologies developed by the start-up

[▼]

A strategy which involves an organisation investing in an interesting start-up company. The investing organisation seeks to nurture the start-up by forming close ties with it

[▼]

Picklist:

Incubate/accelerate strategy
Build strategy
Buy strategy
Partner strategy

---

46   Team A have been working together on a project for three months. At the latest project review meeting it has become apparent that the project scope has begun to increase due to additional requirements from key customers. Team member S states the team needs to focus on the original objectives agreed at the start of the project. Team member B argues that the customer is always right and the team needs to adapt to the new requirements. Team member D wants the project manager to raise the issue with the project sponsor.

According to research on group development by Tuckman, at which stage in the process of group formation has Team A reached?

  ○   The norming stage

  ○   The storming stage

  ○   The forming stage

  ○   The performing stage

---

47   **What is the total time needed for a project if the earliest start time is day 3, the latest finish time is day 25, and the float time is 2 days?**

    ○   28 days

    ○   22 days

    ○   20 days

    ○   27 days

48   Winston Co is a courier delivery company which has recently acquired Deliver Us, a start-up technology firm which has developed the latest parcel tracking software. The board at Winston Co believe that the software developed by Deliver Us will eventually become a piece of industry standard software which will be used by all other courier firms. The board at Winston Co believe that the acquisition of Deliver Us will enable them to capitalise on the sales and profits generated when the new software goes on sale. Winston Co will maintain complete control over the day-to-day activities undertaken by Deliver Us.

    Which of the World Economic Forum's strategies for creating disruptive business models BEST describes the situation involving Winston Co and Deliver Us?

    ○   Partner strategy

    ○   Buy strategy

    ○   Incubate/accelerate strategy

    ○   Invest strategy

49   **Complete the definition of the term operating models using the options below:**

    Operating models describe the key [   ] that exist between an organisation's internal business [   ], [   ] and structures, and the interactions that take place between them. They represent the key [   ] between an organisation's [   ] intentions and the [   ] of that strategy.

    Picklist:

    relationships
    stakeholders
    functions
    processes
    activities
    execution
    conflict
    operational
    implementation
    strategic
    linkage

50 'Establishing a structure of tasks that need to be performed to achieve the goals of the organisation; grouping these tasks into jobs for individuals or teams; allocating jobs to sections and departments; delegating authority to carry out the jobs; providing systems of information and communication.'

Which of Fayol's five functions of a manager is being described above?

- ○ Planning
- ○ Organising
- ○ Co-ordinating
- ○ Commanding

51 SLK and Co is a firm of accountants. SLK and Co employ 30 qualified accountants and three managers to provide accountancy services to clients. SLK and Co offer this group of workers a clear career path with opportunities for professional development and progression. SLK and Co also employs a small team of part-time workers in its payroll team; members of this team will on occasions work overtime as and when required to meet peaks in the workload of the payroll team. SLK and Co will on occasions hire in external providers with specialist knowledge of corporate tax law to assist the firm's clients.

Which of the groups discussed above represents the flexible labour force in Handy's Shamrock?

- ○ The qualified accountants
- ○ The payroll team members
- ○ The external providers
- ○ The three managers

52 Jim is the leader of a small team working in a call centre. A number of team members have complained that Jim often behaves in a cold and distant manner towards them. Jim is reluctant to get involved in team activities and does not like dealing with matters relating to the welfare of team members. Instead Jim is keen for the team to largely run itself.

Which of Lewin et al's styles of leadership describes Jim's approach to leadership?

- ○ Laissez-faire
- ○ Authoritarian
- ○ Task oriented
- ○ Democratic

53 The World Economic Forum identified digital operating models which organisations can use when responding to digital disruption.

Using the options listed below match the correct label against the description of the digital operating model:

A digital operating model which makes extensive use of data analytics and intelligence

A digital operating model which makes use of machines, robotics and artificial intelligence

A digital operating model which is outward looking and is focused on enhancing the organisation's offering

A digital operating model whereby the organisation aims to make its customers' lives easier

Picklist:

Open and liquid
Customer-centric
Data-powered
Skynet

---

54 Jules is member of a five-person project team that is developing a new product. During yesterday's latest project team meeting Bob, a fellow team member, suggested that a number of shortcuts be taken to deliver the new product by the project deadline. Jules highlighted that such action would ultimately lead to a poor quality output which would not be fit for purpose. Bob acknowledged Jules' point, but insisted that hitting the deadline was his sole priority, a view which was supported by the other three team members. Despite feeling uneasy about it Jules reluctantly agreed to support Bob's proposal.

Which of the following common problems of team working describes the approach taken by Jules?

○　The Abilene Paradox

○　Conformity

○　Groupthink

○　Inter-group conflict

---

55 Handy argues that a team's effectiveness depends on three factors.

Which of the following is NOT one of Handy's factors of team effectiveness?

○　Givens

○　Outcomes

○　Intervening factors

○　Dynamics

56   Insight Co (Insight) provides online market research services to a number of multi national companies. Insight makes extensive use of social media analytics tools in order to identify user trends. Insight uses the trends that it identifies to help large companies develop new products and services which appeal to their own customers. Insight places a strong focus on innovation and is constantly seeking to make use of the latest analytics tools. Creative thinking is highly valued at Insight.

Which type of digital operating model has Insight Co adopted using the World Economic Forum's classifications?

- ○   Data-powered
- ○   Open and liquid
- ○   Customer-centric
- ○   Skynet

57   'The body to which the project manager is accountable for achieving project objectives'

Which of the following project stakeholder groups is being described in the statement above?

- ○   The project owner
- ○   The project sponsor
- ○   The project board
- ○   Process stakeholders

58   Daniel, a senior manager in BTT Co, has been appointed to support the work being performed by a project team which is in the process of developing a brand new piece of software which will be used across the organisation. Although not involved in the day-to-day work of the project, Daniel has been asked by the board of directors to represent the project to all the departments in BTT Co. This will involve communicating the vision and objectives of the project and the benefits that the new software will bring.

Which of the following project stakeholder roles BEST matches the role being undertaken by Daniel?

- ○   Project champion
- ○   Project support team member
- ○   Project outcome stakeholder
- ○   Project manager

59 An organisation has just established a project team that consists of departmental members who have been seconded to the project on a full-time basis. The rationale for this approach was that it would enable the team members to devote their time to the project without distraction. Some of the heads of department have raised concerns that they will be short staffed for the duration of the project.

Which type of approach to structuring the project team is being outlined above?

○   Lightweight matrix

○   Heavyweight matrix

○   Balanced model

○   Divisional model

---

60 The rise of digital technologies has resulted in a digital revolution which is affecting many existing businesses and industries.

In order to survive the digital revolution, organisations need to build business models which are:

○   Diverse and ready

○   Strong and stable

○   Disruptive and resilient

○   Creative and changing

Practice mock answers

Answers

1 The correct answers are:

(1)	Define corporate objectives
(2)	Collaboratively define job tasks and responsibilities
(3)	Agree and set specific task objectives
(4)	Agree and set specific key results
(5)	Agree individual performance improvement plans
(6)	Establish system of monitoring, self-evaluation and review of performance against objectives
(7)	Periodic review of performance

2 The correct answer is: Adversarial.

In traditional markets, organisations have tended to take an adversarial approach to the business environments in which they operate. A focus on sharing, collaboration and co-operation are features of ecosystem environments.

3 The correct answer is: The forming stage – The objectives being pursued may as yet be unclear and a leader may not yet have emerged.

The storming stage – There may be changes agreed in the original objectives, procedures and norms established for the group.

The norming stage – Norms and procedures may evolve that enable methodical working to be introduced and maintained.

The performing stage – The team sets to work to execute its task.

4 The correct answers are:

- They allow the employee and their assessor to discuss and agree on personal objectives.
- They provide a system on which salary reviews and promotions can be based.

Reports on employees should be made out in writing and at annual intervals – the intervals at which the appraisal should be carried out depend on the nature of the employee's work. For specialist staff who move from one long-term assignment to another, appraisal may be appropriate after each assignment is completed. For staff engaged in more routine work, an interval of six months or a year may be suitable.

They lead to improvements in performance – criticism of areas where performance has been weak can lead to a defensive response, and future performance may actually deteriorate.

There should be no need to follow up after the interview has taken place – if the system is to be effective, staff must have confidence in it. This will only happen if results are seen to follow from the assessments.

5   The correct answer is: Threat of new entrants.

Porter's five forces model includes the bargaining power of buyers (also known as customers), and the bargaining power of suppliers. It is not specifically focused on the threat posed by new customers or new suppliers. The threat of new stakeholders is incorrect.

6   The correct answer is: Increase resources and increase quality.

The current quality is not acceptable to the HR Director – a key stakeholder in the project. This means significant work is required and therefore additional resource will be needed to meet the deadline in two months' time.

Maintain quality and reduce resources – current quality is not acceptable. Reducing resources would further reduce quality or impact the project completion date.

Reduce resources and increase quality – the quality needs to be improved, but reducing resourse is likely to further reduce quality and impact the project completion deadline.

Increase resources and maintain quality – an increase in resources would ensure the deadline is met for project completion, but existing quality is not acceptable so maintaining at this level will not meet the standards of the new HR Director.

7   The correct answer is: Controlling a stage – the process undertaken by the project manager to ensure that any given stage of the project remains on course.

Directing a project is the responsibility of the senior management team or project board. This process continues throughout the life of the project but is limited to higher aspects of control and decision making.

Initiating a project is an initial planning process that includes quality planning, setting up project controls and creating the project initiation document, which sets fundamental progress and success criteria.

Managing stage boundaries is the process that must be undertaken when a project has more than one stage.

8   The correct answer is: Participants.

The ecosystem concept suggests that stakeholders such as those mentioned should be viewed as participants.

9   The correct answers are:

- Profession – the student is studying engineering and working in an engineering manufacturing environment.
- Type of business – manufacturing culture based on output results meeting specification
- Organisational – the student will have to participate in the corporate culture, which will be heavily influenced by the national culture in China.

Culture can be discussed on many different levels. The 'category' or 'group' of people whose shared behaviours and meanings may constitute a culture include:

A nation, region or ethnic group

Women versus men ('gender culture')

A social class (eg 'working class culture')

A profession or occupation

A type of business (eg 'advertising culture')

An organisation ('organisational culture')

10   The correct answer is: 3 days.

Latest finish time is day 21, require 15 days to complete: 21 − 15 = 6

Earliest start time is day 3: 6 − 3 = 3

11   The correct answer is:

- Rules
- Connections
- Course of interactions

Role, reach and capability are the three distinct components that make up ecosystem participants according to Davidson et al.

12   The correct answers are:

- Perceptual selection
- Jargon
- Selective reporting

Perceptual selection. People hearing only what they want to hear in a message.

Jargon. People from different job or specialist backgrounds (eg HR managers and IT experts) can have difficulty in talking on a non-specialist's wavelength.

Selective reporting. Subordinates may give superiors incorrect or incomplete information (eg to protect a colleague or to avoid 'bothering' the superior). A senior manager may, however, only be able to handle edited information because they do not have time to sift through details.

Encoding refers to the process of transferring the information the sender wishes to send into a given form, for example putting information into words.

Decoding is the stage where the receiver processes the message into meaning.

Informal communication can furnish emotional and social support to an individual, improving communication.

13   The correct answer is: Avoid.

There is a high probability of this software causing an issue as it has already been identified that it does not meet the requirements. There are legal implications to not securing customer data effectively, and the potential for payment details to be stolen means the impact could be extensive and expensive. A new software package needs to be identified and used for the payment element of the website.

The other options were as follows:

Reduction or mitigation are those measures taken to reduce the likelihood and/or the consequences of the risk event. This would not appear to be possible in this situation.

Transference. The risk is passed on to, or shared with, another party (eg an insurer). The risk of customer payment details becoming lost would be too significant to be transferred to another party.

Absorption. The potential risk is accepted in the hope or expectation that the incidence and consequences can be coped with if necessary. This would not appear to be possible in this situation.

14   The correct answers are:

Completing tasks according to the schedule	**Execution**
Ensuring the project meets the goals	**Project completion**
Setting project goals and objectives	**Initiation**
Recruiting the project manager	**Planning**
Measuring project progress	**Control**

15   The correct answer is: Orchestrator.

Where the activities undertaken by those participants in an ecosystem are formally co-ordinated by another participant, this party is known as the ecosystem orchestrator. The role of the orchestrator will not always be performed by a commercial entity in the ecosystem but may be performed by a government body or regulator.

16   The correct answer is: Planning is not a constraint; it is a process that may be carried out at any time in order to satisfy the requirements of other processes.

17   The correct answer is: Introducing a training programme for existing managers.

According to Herzberg's hygiene-motivation theory, hygiene factors are essential and therefore expected to be in place by the workforce. Absence of one or more hygiene factors will cause dissatisfaction. Introduction of motivational factors will only increase satisfaction if all hygiene factors are satisfied.

Currently at RSJ Construction, a key hygiene factor that is absent is the quality of supervision, and this means that the most immediate aspect to be rectified is to improve the quality of supervision by training the existing management team.

18   The correct answer is: Do not indicate the need for resources to be co-ordinated.

19   The correct answer is: High degree of complexity and loose orchestration.

A shark tank ecosystem has a low degree of complexity and loose orchestration.

A wolf pack ecosystem has a low degree of complexity and tight orchestration.

A lion's pride ecosystem has a high degree of complexity and tight orchestration.

20   The correct answer is: Control gate.

Control gates represent key points in the project's life cycle that allow the project sponsor or steering committee the opportunity to review project progress and make a decision as to whether to continue with, or terminate, the project.

21   The correct answer is: Setting organisational policies and procedures.

Planning departmental budgets and monitoring the performance of work teams are associated with the tactical control level. Processing invoices is an operational-level control.

22   The correct answers are:

- Scheduling employee shifts
- Dealing with customer complaints

Recruitment of factory managers and meeting with new suppliers are part of the tactical (functional) level of control.

Dealing with corporate governance issues is part of the corporate-level strategy.

23   The correct answer is: Determine value.

The four stages involved in the process of value creation are:

Stage 1: Define value
Stage 2: Create value
Stage 3: Deliver value
Stage 4: Capture value

24   The correct answers are:

| Mr A | Plant |
| Mr B | Completer-finisher |

25   The correct answers are:

		Horizontal	Vertical
(a)	Use of an integrated computer system	✓	
(b)	Operating separate bonus schemes for the sales force administrative staff and management		✓
(c)	Increase in staff union membership		✓
(d)	Reduction in headcount across the organisation	✓	
(e)	Staff managers encroaching on the roles of line managers	✓	

Horizontal conflict between individuals and groups at the same broad level in the organisation. This is often based on competition for limited influence and resources.

Vertical conflict between different levels in the organisation hierarchy. This is often based on conflict of interest and power imbalance.

26   The correct answer is: Residual value.

Capturing value effectively involves the organisation taking a slice of the value that it has created when it is shared with other stakeholders such as shareholders. This is referred to as residual value.

27   The correct answer is: The Abilene Paradox.

Group members accept an idea they don't like in the belief that everybody else supports it. In reality, nobody does.

28   The correct answer is: Accommodating.

Avoiding – withdraw from the conflict

Accommodating – concede the issue to the other person, regardless of your own legitimate concerns

Competing – insist on your own concerns at the expense of others

Compromising – trade concessions through bargaining, negotiating and conciliating, so that each party makes some concessions in order to obtain some gains

The other conflict handling strategy not mentioned in the question relates to collaborating.

Collaborating – working together with the other party in an attempt to find an outcome in which the assertively-stated needs of both parties are met as far as possible

29   The correct answer is: Salary.

30   The correct answer is: Diagonal.

This is interdepartmental communication by people of different ranks.

31 The correct answer is: 1. Identification of relevant stakeholders, 2. Ranking and prioritisation, 3. Identification of the needs of the highest priority stakeholders, 4. Formulation of value propositions.

32 The correct answers are:

Persuasion **differs to** influence as it is always of a direct and **deliberate** nature. Persuasion is aligned to a particular objective which can only be achieved by **gaining** the support of others. Persuasion is not the same as **commanding** a person to do something, as it focuses on reaching agreement.

33 The correct answer is: Add resource – if capable staff are available and it is practicable to add more people to certain tasks, it may be possible to recover some lost ground.

With only a month to go, it is unlikely that rescheduling at this stage will make much difference. If the specification is unrealistic this should have been identified much earlier, so this is also unlikely to be an option now. Doing nothing will mean that the project deadlines are not met and so this is also not an option.

34 The correct answer is: Structured training programmes – these should reduce resistance to change.

35 The correct answer is: Referent – based on force of personality, or 'charisma', which can attract, influence or inspire other people.

Both directors will have reward, legitimate and expert power.

36 The correct answer is: As a tangible unique resource.

As the diamond mines are exclusively owned by the company they cannot be accessed or used by competing firms. As such the mines bestow a competitive advantage on the company as only they can benefit from the diamonds that are mined.

37 The correct answer is: Focus on personal interactions and relationship building – this is an advantage of oral and face-to-face communication because of the ability to build rapport and be sensitive to the audience's needs and responses.

38 The correct answers are:

- The company's code of ethics available on Iceberg City's website
- The company's statement of values and beliefs available on Iceberg City's social media page

Overt aspects of organisational culture are visible as they are documented and therefore even outsiders should be aware of them. Sandeep should have been aware of these before joining the company, especially as these were publicly available.

Covert aspects are not directly in control of management and Sandeep would not become aware of these until she has worked within the organisation. These include informal communications, employee attitudes and structures.

39 The correct answer is: Socio-demographic.

Socio-demographic segmentation is based on social, economic and demographic variables which include age, religion, sex, ethnicity, income, social class, occupation, family size, and education.

40   The correct answers are:

Conflict handling strategies: *Level of assertiveness and importance of the relationship:*

Competing	High: Assertiveness/Low: Importance placed on the relationship
Avoiding	Low: Assetiveness/Low: Importance placed on the relationship
Collaborating	High: Assertiveness/High: Importance placed on the relationship

41   The correct answer is: Groupthink.

A strong culture of self-belief means that ideas generated by the group are not critically evaluated.

42   The correct answer is: Keep informed stakeholder group.

Stakeholders should be kept informed of the organisation's plans. While they may have low power their high interest in the affairs of the organisation increases the scope for them to influence more powerful stakeholder groups to exert influence over the organisation, and they should therefore be treated as a keep informed stakeholder group.

43   The correct answers are:

- Specialist skills – a team might exist to combine expertise from different departments.
- Power in the wider organisation – team members may have influence.

44   The correct answer is: Implementation – Using allocated resources to complete the tasks according to the schedule.

45   The correct answers are:

A strategy which involves an organisation developing its internal capabilities and infrastructures so that it can change the way it currently operates.	**Build strategy**
A strategy which involves an established organisation working with a digital disruptor to learn about the markets that it serves, and the products and services that it provides.	**Partner strategy**
A strategy which involves an established organisation acquiring a digital start-up business. Acquiring a digital start-up enables the organisation to gain access to the innovative technologies developed by the start-up.	**Buy strategy**
A strategy which involves an organisation investing in an interesting start-up company. The investing organisation seeks to nurture the start-up by forming close ties with it.	**Incubate/accelerate strategy**

The only option not included in the question was the invest strategy which involves investing in potentially interesting start-up companies. Unlike a buy strategy an invest strategy leaves the start-up independent from the investing organisation.

46   The correct answer is: The storming stage

There may be changes agreed in the original objectives, procedures and norms established for the group.

The forming stage – The objectives being pursued may as yet be unclear and a leader may not yet have emerged.

The norming stage – Norms and procedures may evolve that enable methodical working to be introduced and maintained.

The performing stage – The team sets to work to execute its task.

47   The correct answer is: 20 days

Latest finish time is day 25 and earliest start time is day 3: 25 – 3 = 22

Float time is 2 days: 22 – 2 = 20

48   The correct answer is: Buy strategy.

The situation outlined in the question describes a buy strategy. The fact that Winston Co had acquired Deliver Us, a start-up technology firm, to gain access to its innovative parcel tracking software should have given you a clue. You may have been tempted to think that it was an invest or incubate/accelerate strategy; however, the distinguishing clue was the mention of Winston Co having complete control over the day-to-day activities of Deliver Us which made it a buy strategy.

49   The correct answer is:

Operating models describe the key **relationships** that exist between an organisation's internal business **functions, processes** and structures, and the interactions that take place between them. They represent the key **linkage** between an organisation's **strategic** intentions and the **execution** of that strategy.

50   The correct answer is: Organising.

Planning involves determining objectives, and strategies, policies, programmes and procedures for achieving those objectives, for the organisation and its sub-units.

Co-ordinating involves harmonising the goals and activities of individuals and groups within the organisation. Management must reconcile differences in approach, effort, interest and timing, in favour of overall (or 'super-ordinate') shared goals.

Commanding involves giving instructions to subordinates to carry out tasks, for which the manager has authority (to make decisions) and responsibility (for performance).

51   The correct answer is: The payroll team members.

The flexible labour force include temporary and part-time workers who can be brought in as and when needed – especially to meet peaks in the demand for services (since they have to be supplied in 'real time'). Their commitment is typically focused on the immediate job and work group, rather than career or the organisation.

The qualified accountants and three managers represent the professional core. This group are the permanently employed people who represent the distinctive knowledge and competences of the firm. They are qualified professionals, technicians and managers. Their commitment is focused on their work and career within the organisation.

The external providers represent the contractual fringe and include freelancers, consultants and subcontractors who are able to undertake non-core activities and/or provide specialist services more economically than the firm could manage internally.

52   The correct answer is: Laissez-faire.

Authoritarian and democratic are the other two leadership styles proposed by Lewin et al.

Task oriented was a distractor and relates to the work of Blake and Mouton.

BPP
LEARNING
MEDIA

53   The correct answers are:

A digital operating model which makes extensive use of data analytics and intelligence.	Data-powered
A digital operating model which makes use of machines, robotics and artificial intelligence	Skynet
A digital operating model which is outward looking and is focused on enhancing the organisation's offering	Open and liquid
A digital operating model whereby the organisation aims to make its customers' lives easier	Customer-centric

The other digital operating model put forward by the World Economic Forum is the Xtra-Frugal model which requires the organisation to develop a 'less is more' culture, and to optimise its internal processes. The formulation of a centralised organisational structure is a common feature of this.

54   The correct answer is: Conformity.

Conformity. Individuals are pressured to agree with the majority against their better judgement. This would appear to best describe the approach taken by Jules.

The Abilene Paradox. An unpopular plan is implemented because each member thinks that they are the only one who doesn't support it and therefore keeps quiet.

Groupthink. The team is so confident in its abilities that it does not critically evaluate its decisions.

Inter-group conflicts may become an obstruction.

55   The correct answer is: Dynamics.

Handy argues that a team's effectiveness depends on:

Givens: ie the team, the task and the environment

Intervening factors: ie the leadership style, procedures and motivation levels

Outcomes: ie the productivity of the group and satisfaction of members

Dynamics is not one of Handy's three factors. Dynamics relates to the level of change and history of success or failure.

56   The correct answer is: Data-powered.

The data-powered digital operating model makes extensive use of data analytics and intelligence. This is evident as Insight makes use of social media analytics tools to identify user trends, which it then uses to help large companies develop new products and services. The mention of having an innovative culture where creativity is valued is a common characteristic of the data-powered digital operating model.

57   The correct answer is: The project board.

The project owner: Is the person for whom the project is being carried out (eg a client or senior manager).

The project sponsor: Provides, and is accountable for, the resources invested into the project and is responsible for the achievement of the project's business objectives.

Process stakeholders: Have an interest in how the project process is conducted (eg those involved in it).

58 The correct answer is: Project champion.

The project champion represents the project to the rest of the organisation, communicating its vision and objectives, and securing commitment and resources. This is the role that Daniel is undertaking.

Project support team members refer to the personnel working on a project who do not report directly to the project manager. This is not applicable as Daniel is not involved in the day-to-day work of the project team.

Project outcome stakeholders have an interest in the outcomes, results or deliverables (eg users of a new system). This may apply to Daniel in part as he is a senior manager at BTT Co, and will want the project to deliver a successful outcome. However, as the question specifically asked for the best match, the correct answer is project champion.

59 The correct answer is: Heavyweight matrix.

The lightweight, heavyweight and balanced model are different types of matrix structure.

The lightweight matrix involves the project manager co-ordinating the project and chairing meetings between the departments involved. However, the project manager has limited power to enforce the commitment of departmental members.

The balanced model involves a department being incentivised to engage with a project by linking part of the department's income to the successful completion of that project. While this increases the power of the project manager, it can create conflict between departmental needs and project needs.

The divisional model was a distractor.

60 The correct answer is: Disruptive and resilient.

The need for disruptive and resilient business models requires organisations to undertake strategies which disrupt existing ways of working even if they result in short-term upheaval.